From Flood

From Flood To Flood

Ten Tumultuous Years for an Historic Devon Market Town, 1970-1979

Newton Abbot repeatedly hit the headlines in a decade when everything changed – its events faithfully recorded by local weekly newspaper the Mid-Devon Advertiser

Brian Thomas

℗ 2023

The right of Brian Thomas to be identified as the author of this work has been asserted in accordance with sections 77 and 78 of the Copyright Designs and Patents Act 1988. All rights reserved. No part of this manuscript may be reproduced, stored in a retrieval system, or transmitted in any form or by any means, electronic, mechanical, photocopying, recording, or otherwise, without the prior permission of the author.

Parts of this book were previously published as *Newton Abbot in the News* by Obelisk Publications of Exeter in 1998 and has been out of print for many years. It has been extensively revamped by the author in 2023 and every effort has been made to ensure the accuracy of the contents. Any errors are probably mine, with the exception of inaccuracies published in period newspapers and reiterated in good faith.

This book it especially dedicated to
publisher Chips Barber
editor George Taylor
and town and district councillor Mrs Di Nicholls.
Without whom…

Most of the archive photographs used are courtesy of the *Mid-Devon Advertiser* and special thanks are extended especially to the paper's Editor at the time, George Taylor, as well as all the reporters who served the title in the 1970s and, particularly, its talented photographic team of Arthur Kay and Rex Hitchcock – not to overlook long-time contributor, the late A. Vincent Bibbings, who submitted many images to the paper over the years, including (herein): Newton Abbot's power station seen up river from the Passage House Inn, the cycling milkman from 1970 and his much-publicised 1938 flood pictures. Also, Newton Abbot rail bridge, Mark S. Wilkins; period Sandford Orleigh interior pictures, courtesy Mrs Betty Matthews; Avro Canada's 1950s VZ-9-AV Avrocar, from *Popular Mechanics*; Yes covers Hipgnosis; Chips and Sally Barber photo, courtesy Sally Barber; Owen Caunter quote from *Along The Lemon* by Judy Chard, first published by Bossiney Books in 1978, 1993 edition Orchard Publications. Attempts have been made to track down any possible outstanding illustration copyright holders.

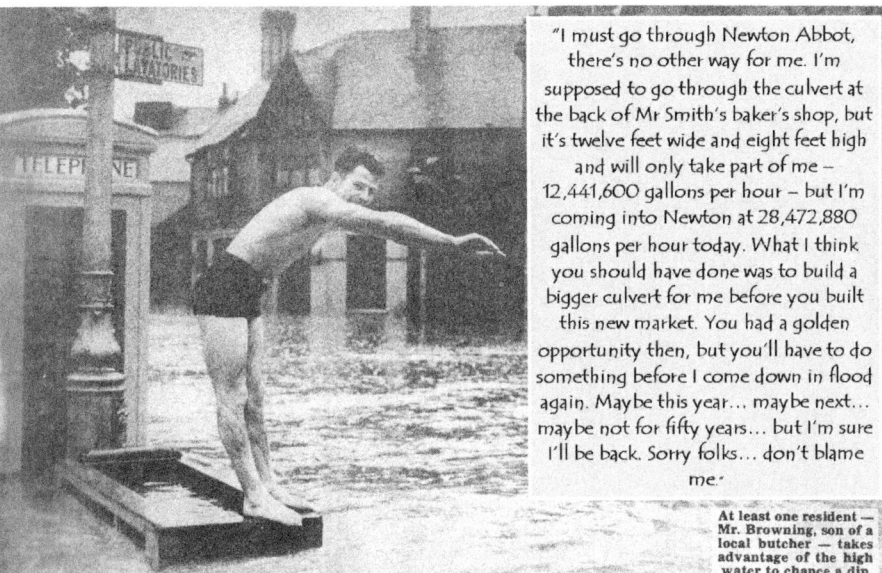

"I must go through Newton Abbot, there's no other way for me. I'm supposed to go through the culvert at the back of Mr Smith's baker's shop, but it's twelve feet wide and eight feet high and will only take part of me – 12,441,600 gallons per hour – but I'm coming into Newton at 28,472,880 gallons per hour today. What I think you should have done was to build a bigger culvert for me before you built this new market. You had a golden opportunity then, but you'll have to do something before I come down in flood again. Maybe this year... maybe next... maybe not for fifty years... but I'm sure I'll be back. Sorry folks... don't blame me."

At least one resident — Mr. Browning, son of a local butcher — takes advantage of the high water to chance a dip

A judicious warning to councillors and their chiefs about Newton Abbot's potential future came from the 'lips' of the River Lemon itself, as told by Chipley Bridge resident Owen Caunter after the 1979 flooding of the town.

The bloated river had swept through the Caunter home in a similar catastrophe 41 years earlier in 1938 "and spoilt all his furniture" and he feared more of the same for the decades to come.

His Lemontations were right.

Those watercourse reflections of his, entitled *I am a River – it Wasn't my Fault*, formed a fitting climax to local author Judy Chard's most renowned and timely 1979 book, *Along the Lemon*.

The newspaper photo above shows the torrent that struck in 1938: a posed image with a light-hearted twist as, clearly, the water wasn't deep enough for that kind of plunge. But a nice, atmospheric set-up for the camera by master lens-man, A. Vincent Bibbings.

Tales from the Decade
And where you can find them…

Newton Abbot – What you may or may not know 1
Introduction to a Decade of Changes 5
Strike! 7
Out-of-Town Mania: Trago, Dickies, Plymco, Tesco 9
The Market and the Multi-Storey 13
Constructing the new market complex, 1975 20
Denbury Camp/Channings Wood Prison 22
The 'Devil's' Faithful 25
Feted Yachtsman 26
Hustling on the Hustings 27
Top Estate 27
Bradley Mills, the Vicarys, Dyrons and the Penn Inn Pool 28
Disk Sockey 32
Of Hovercraft and Hydrofoils: Forde Park School 33
Just One Pint Today, Please… 35
Snippets #1 36
Sandford Orleigh – and the lady who was nearly a slave 39
Furled 43
New Stations 44
Excuse me, Ma'am 45
What's in a Name – Lemon? 46
'Tiny' 47
Streaking 48
No Power for the People 49
Keep Our Casualty Unit! 54
The Family Department Store 56
Poles Apart 57

A Towering Pageant 58
New Council – Ancient House 60
The Passmore Edwards Ownership Tussle 62
Is There a Doctor in the House? 64
Old Town Hall, But New Courthouse 66
Snippets #2 68
The Spin of the Globe 69
Donkeys' Ears 70
A Priest's House – or Not – and the Squandered Stones 71
Local Publishers Hit "Rocky Patch" 74
Merry-Go-Roundabout 77
Of Pantomime Horses and Liverpool Merchants: TV Comedy comes to Newton Abbot 78
The By-Pass From Hell 80
The Bridge That Went Down in a Day 82
Vroom! That Was the Queen, That Was 83
It Wasn't You… 85
The Leper Home 86
Coffee Break 87
On Our Bikes 88
Bailing In 90
Snippets #3 – the Musical Notes 91
Tanks For the Memories 92
Crossing Now – Seven Elephants 93
New Lamps For Old 94
Decoy Park: Hovercrafty… Plus: A Lake? No, Thank you 95
Badge of Flowers 96
Royal Accolade for Newton Writer 97
Snippets #4 98

Giving Up the Ghost 99
Keep Watching the Skies 101
The Last Great Flood 104
Postscript: 114
The Final Pieces 117
'Chips' Barber 119
Paul Theroux 121
Cllr Mrs Di Nicholls 123
The Mid-Devon Advertiser 127
Yes… 132
About the Author 133
Museum 137

The Alexandra Theatre (advertising the controversial film A Clockwork Orange*), with the multi-storey car park behind (left), the former Bradley Hotel (now The Jolly Farmer) to the right and the old power station on the skyline, taken 1970s*

Newton Abbot
What you may or may not know

Queen Street, probably pictured in the 1950s, with its packed pavements, on-street parking and **two-way** *traffic (including a double-decker bus)! Though now pedestrianised, the busy street seems somehow narrower these days. Or did we just have thinner cars, buses and pedestrians post-war?*

NEWTON ABBOT has been a thriving market town since the early 13th century. Traces of Iron Age hill forts have been found both at Berry's Wood, dating back to the 7th century BC, and Milber Downs, dating back to the 1st century BC – an area later occupied by the Romans.

It was originally two towns. In 1220 the area south of the River Lemon was owned by the Abbey of Torre and was granted the right to hold weekly markets and an annual fair on its land. As the town thrived, it became known as Newton (new-town) Abbot. In 1246, the Bushel family, who owned the north area of the river, also gained rights to hold markets and annual fairs and their territory became Newton Bushel.

The town's iconic landmark, St Leonards Tower, was built in the 13th century by the Abbots of Torre as a chapel. In 1688, an announcement was read in front of the chapel to tell the gathered crowd that Prince William of Orange was claiming the English monarchy, despite James II still being on the throne.

Wool and leather industries flourished during the mediaeval period, and centuries later, the clay industry boomed. In 1663 the markets and fairs were combined, and eventually moved to Newton Abbot – a decision of the Yarde Family, who built Bradley Manor in the early 15th century, now a National Trust property. The Union Bridge was formed to link Newton Abbot and Newton Bushel in 1822 and the two communities were finally joined under one local authority in 1901.

Newton Abbot Racecourse was established in 1866 and the town's population grew from a few thousand to over 12,500 in the 19th century. The Great Western Railway came to town in 1846 when the existing line was extended from Teignmouth and extensive repair yards operated here until their relocation to Plymouth in 1970. A fascinating display of the history of steam in the town – along with an original working signal gantry from the town's rail station – can be viewed at the town museum at Newton's Place, on the corner of Wolborough Street.

Opposite the rail station, the pastoral Courtenay Park was laid out in 1854, with the bandstand opening in 1907. Queen Elizabeth visited troops there in 1952, just before her coronation. The striking Renaissance-style Passmore Edwards public library was designed by Victorian architect Sylvanus Trevail in honour of Edward Passmore's mother, who was born in the town. Passmore originally wanted to build a hospital, but the town already had one, opened in 1904, and this has now been moved to contemporary premises in Jetty Marsh Road with its former East Street site redeveloped with retail and housing units.

Among the many famous faces associated with the town over the years are diving salvage innovator John Lethbridge (a to-scale model of his extraordinary underwater craft hangs from the ceiling of the town museum), theatrical architect Frank Matcham, explorer Sir Samuel White Baker, the first woman to be called to the English bar, Ivy Williams, and early film actress Norah Baring (who appeared in the 1930 Alfred Hitchcock-directed talkie, *Murder!* Also noted are international cricketer

Len Coldwell, TV sports presenter David Vine and rock band Kasabian's guitarist Sergio Pizzorno. Not forgetting that in 1908 Emmeline Pankhurst and her daughter visited Newton Abbot to campaign for votes for women.

Still, we're here to look at the Nineteen Seventies, so let's press on…

The Mid-Devon Advertiser of December 1979, summed up the end of the outgoing decade like this.

"Robert Louis Stevenson once observed that 'by the time man gets well into his seventies his existence is a mere miracle.'

"Certainly those of us who have managed to survive the **1970s** might well consider that *our* continued existence was a miracle.

"Now that the Christmas pudding has finally settled and the slings and arrows of 1970 have faded into hopes for the new decade, we can look back with relief on ten years of technological advancement and trouble and strife…"

Introduction to a Decade of Changes

Lemon Road: hit by the first of two major Seventies floods, this in 1970

THE NINETEEN SEVENTIES began inspirationally with the first Moon landing and ended forebodingly with a fuel crisis, inflation and unemployment. It was a technological decade that saw microprocessors, solar energy and test tube babies, the first flights of supersonic aircraft Concorde and a growth of nuclear reactors.

There was also widespread industrial unrest, strikes, food shortages, the infamous three-day week, four general elections and the first invites to join a European Parliament. Decimal coinage was introduced, local government was streamlined and Queen Elizabeth II celebrated her Silver Jubilee.

The ten tumultuous years were decisive for Newton Abbot in terms of social and geographic change.

The way Newtonians shopped, travelled, lived and worked took significant turns between the start of 1970 and the end of 1979.

Famous buildings disappeared, a new market complex was built, the Newton by-pass was constructed; a new district council took over, ending the old Urban/Rural split, and big chain stores laid the groundwork for out-of-town food centres that would blossom in the Eighties.

Intermediate Area Development Status, providing European finance for important industrial projects, was granted to the new district after years of struggle in the Seventies, only for it to be lost again in the Eighties.

The decade began with South Devon's longest strike, its first of two devastating floods, and ended with an even worse flood – and, between the two, ironically suffered a serious drought in 1976.

Residents celebrated the history of Newton Abbot's internationally-famous St Leonard's Tower, saw well-known faces come and go and new roads built in a flurry of apparently never-ending activity.

Strike!

As the chill winter winds ushered in a new decade, the most protracted strike in South Devon's history was entering its third week. The bitter 20-week stoppage over a wages dispute at Newton Abbot engineering firm Centrax also hit the company's factories at Heathfield and Exeter.

Violence flared on the picket lines in January and the steep and narrow Haccombe Path became packed with police vehicles. The one thousand employees were warned that the company might close but, after an acrimonious conflict, a new wages structure was agreed in March.

Founded in 1946 to manufacture industrial gas turbines, the company moved to Newton Abbot ten years later when it also began producing jet engine turbine blades, gears and axles. Its export performance was so good that in 1967 the Minister of State at the

Board of Trade, Lord Brown, asked Totnes MP Ray Mawby to make an official visit – though that was also threatened with strike action.

A 70-acre site in Shaldon Road was chosen for the 240,000 sq ft factory in the 1950s after negotiations collapsed for land at Forches Cross, site of the 1952 Royal Agricultural Show, and permission was given for the works in December 1954 by Devon Planning Committee. About 75 per cent of the chosen site overlooking the River Teign was originally woodland from which a large amount of timber was taken during 1914-18 to aid the war effort.

The 1970s decade was one of hostile industrial confrontations, slumps in orders, redundancies, takeover rumours, recriminations and short-time working. (The Fifties and Sixties had been little better, with 104 laid off in 1957 and 91 in 1961, for example). But some of the animosity eased in 1976 through a new spirit of co-operation, though periodic upheavals still continued. In 1993 an ambitious proposal for an adjoining business park was put on hold – as Teignbridge Council felt it was premature until the Penn Inn flyover was built (finally completed in 2016) – and in 1994 a £4.5 million contract for Rover helped secure around 160 Centrax jobs.

Out-of-Town Mania: Trago, Dickies, Plymco, Tesco

Crowds queued and a band played for the opening of Dickie's Discounts in 1974

Opened in 1968, Trago Mills cash and carry, then a group of huts on a boggy lowland site close to Heathfield, probably set the scene for later out-of-town stores that would cause controversy in the area throughout the Seventies and finally take control over the next decade and beyond.

It was revealed by Devon County Council in January 1970 that the public inquiry into the Trago development, held the previous November, cost £5,035. In July 1971 Trago won a four and a half year battle to formally establish its out-of-town shopping centre at Liverton, and in September 1974 an out-of-town food store, Dickie's Discounts, opened on the site. In July 1975 Tesco began its local foray into the decentralised store market when the company announced plans for a 90,000 sq ft hypermarket at Heathfield, which it lost on appeal in March 1977. In August 1977 the company applied for a superstore on the site of the Dutton Foreshaw garage, opposite the racecourse. But the plan was refused by Teignbridge Council in November that year by a 13-8 vote after a three-hour debate.

A similar plan by the Co-op involving the old laundry building in Newton Road was also rejected by councillors, by 14-1. But in January 1978 the company announced plans to fight the decision and in March the council gave the go-ahead for a 30,000 sq ft Co-op store in Kingsteignton. The Homemaker branch opened in August 1990.

Back with Tesco: In August 1978 the chain unveiled its plan for the racecourse-facing site which Teignbridge rejected by 22 votes to five in October. A public inquiry was held in March 1979 which the company won on appeal and district planners approved details of the project in February 1981. The 55,000 sq ft Tesco store was finally opened in Newton Road on 3 August, 1982 – and out-of-town shopping had finally arrived.

Returning to the Co-op: The group contemplated building a superstore in Forde Road in the mid-Eighties. Instead, it opened its controversial £8 million, 40,000 sq ft Plymco on the site of the popular Penn Inn swimming pool and park on 24 October, 1989 – won on appeal against bitter opposition. Its old local headquarters in Queen Street, Newton House, built in 1937 on the site of four houses and extended to a three-storey department store in 1972, closed in June 1990.

The public fight to resist both the Newton Road Tesco and the Penn Inn Plymco were both hostile and protracted, with the latter taking a particularly sour twist because of the loss of leisure facilities that had once been gifted to the town.

As a footnote: Normans Superwarehouses opened at the Trago complex in July 1988 in a building designed like a mediaeval castle; in July 1995 the Co-op bought the business.

WHEN a lorry driver told Newton Abbot County Court that he had been travelling at about 25mph at the time of an accident, the Registrar, Mr C. A. Munro, commented: "Every accident I have ever dealt with happens at 25mph!"

Even so, the court upheld the lorry driver's claim for £182 damages, and a counter-claim by the driver of a car was dismissed.

The Market and the Multi-Storey

Newton Abbot's market complex underwent a major upheaval in the 1970s with the building of an eight-deck concrete car park and construction of a new shopping centre, Market Walk.

Changes began in 1970 when it was announced that a multi-storey car park was to be erected on the site of the sheep and cattle markets in Sherborne Road. Opposition to the project began in March of that year, but the proposal went ahead. Construction work was swift, and on 9 June the sheep and pig markets returned to their old site from temporary pens in Market Square– but relocated underneath the new car park.

The 362-vehicle multi-storey building finally opened for business on Monday 13 December, 1971, and served just 36 cars up to lunchtime. But, by the end of the first week, 1,168 had rolled up the snaking ramp to use it. It was formally opened on 1 February, 1972, by Urban District Council chairman Cllr Leonard Lamb. After the ceremony, involving both the car park and the new sheep and pig market below deck one, Cllr Lamb and members of the civic party were whisked off to inspect the roof deck in a Rolls Royce.

The car park cost £238,260 and the livestock section £40,071, equipped with pens for 1,230 sheep and 510 pigs with a reserve of 310 pens. A pedestrian bridge was added to the multi-storey on 15 October, 1978 and a £50,000 refurbishment was undertaken in 1993/94, including shifting the lift to the front elevation and adding an outside stairway between the roof and the bridge deck.

UDC planning committee chairman Cllr L.A. Daymond points out details on a model of the proposed centre redevelopment in 1970

Plans for the long-awaited town centre redevelopment were unveiled in October, 1970. Sketches, maps, models and artists' impressions went on public display at The Avenue Methodist Church. The scheme involved the acquisition of seventeen acres of land and compulsory purchase orders on numerous business premises, including long-lived gentlemen's outfitters Laws and Wareham, adjacent to Lloyds Bank. A covered precinct was proposed with a traffic-free centre of 60,000 sq ft.

The site for the multi-storey car park (centre, left) and long-gone Sherborne Road car park with its beloved plane trees (top left), pictured in January 1970

The decision to fell a line of plane trees at the rear of Lloyds Bank, which were in the way of the development, caused indignation among traders and shoppers alike in September 1971, but they were axed anyway. Among the buildings to disappear were the old slipper baths, fire station and Chicken Café.

A 10,000-signature petition was submitted to the Urban District Council in January 1971 in a fight to keep a Romart store out of Newton Abbot town centre and the proposal was subsequently thrown out by councillors. In September 1974 four companies started bidding for the redevelopment contract and Taylor Woodrow was successful. But market traders were almost unanimously opposed to the project, warning that it would kill the town market. In May 1976 they organised a convoy of protest around the town, led by a coffin and three women dressed in mourning black and carrying memorial crosses.

A three-day inquiry into the road closures necessary for the market square scheme to go ahead was held in September 1976; the market stalls moved to Victoria Place in May 1977 to allow work to begin, and on 27 June the £2.25 million redevelopment finally got underway. Taylor Woodrow worked first on the main unit,

International Stores, then moved clockwise around the site towards Courtenay Street and the Boots unit and out towards the old Post Office in Bearnes Lane.

Stalls in Victoria Place, 1977, a time when there was no Albany Street doctors' surgery and the town still had a bus station (left, across the river)

Stallholders spent their last trading days in the old market hall in April 1978; a hiccough with the terrazzo flooring in the refurbished building delayed their return (it did not set properly and needed re-laying), but most of them celebrated their homecoming in November 1978 and a sign on the wall said it all: WELCOME BACK, WE'VE MISSED YOU.

Market Walk had been chosen as the name for the new complex in a *Mid-Devon Advertiser* competition in August 1978 and the new market square opened on 21 February, 1979. One of the first responses was that it was 'cramped' for stallholders.

It was district councillors' time to quibble three months later when they turned out for the official opening on 11 May only to be barred from joining a following buffet lunch in the Butter Market. A hoarding was unveiled by county vice-chairman Cllr John Martin and district chairman Cllr Leslie Pike to mark the end of the exhausting four-way project involving TDC, DCC, Taylor Woodrow and Standard Life.

Taylor Woodrow chairman John Topping was heckled with shouts of "It's a shambles!" and "Build homes, not shops!" and the chairman of the Market Traders' Association boycotted the event as he, along with the MTA secretary and the chairman of the Chamber of Trade, had neglectfully not been invited to the ceremony until 4.30pm the day before.

Exactly one month later, on 11 June, a burst pipe caused a five foot chunk of the food hall ceiling to collapse, showering an estimated 200 gallons of water over stalls and around market day shoppers. It happened at peak shopping time, 11.45am, directly over the dairy produce stall of Mrs Mary Symons, and at one point the sudden downpour rested at three inches deep. A burst joint on a pressure main was responsible with an initial leak building up in an 80ft section of the ceiling before discharge.

The Post Office transferred from its old premises in Bearnes Lane at the end of August and re-opened in the market square on 1 October; the old building was demolished to make way for one of two bookend service yards for the new market complex and work then commenced on a new post office sorting office in Highweek Street (a large, purpose-built replacement is now based in Forde Road). Courtenay Street was re-opened as a pedestrianised precinct in August 1993.

The market was founded by Royal Charter in 1269 and was originally held on a Friday, and not a Wednesday. The Alexandra Hall and Butter Market was built in 1871, the hall was extended as a corn exchange and in 1885 converted into a theatre; it was named after Princess Alexandra, wife of Edward VII, who visited Newton Abbot in the late 1800s and stayed at Sandford Orleigh. Changes continued at the town market in 2023 with Teignbridge Council's radical and unpopular plans to create a multi-screen cinema in the market square, replacing the Alexandra's big screen functions, and also removing the theatrical entertainment element of the Grade II listed Devonian Limestone building in order to convert it for commercial use, extending the floor space of the existing market hall.

Entertainer Leslie Crowther ("Crackerjack!") opened International Stores in Market Walk in November 1978.
The company was leaving its former Queen Street store, ironically in its Jubilee Year.
It came to the town in 1895 and moved to Queen Street in 1918.
Its replacement building is now a branch of Wilko.

Constructing the new market complex, 1975

Above: Ground works for International Stores begins.

Next page:

1, International Stores rises;

2, the fated car park and its plane trees (*left*) plus the partly-demolished properties between the narrow road that ran parallel to the car park and behind Courtenay Street premises;

3, the former slipper baths (*centre*).

Denbury Camp/Channings Wood Prison

Denbury Camp, December 1970

Denbury Camp, on the outskirts of Newton Abbot, became redundant to the Ministry of Defence in 1969 and after being closed for nearly a year it became largely forgotten.

That is until the Home Office announced its decision in February 1970 to turn the 90-acre site into a prison. The outcry was loud and fierce.

The place was built as a 'rush job' in 1938 by the War Office which urgently needed a conscription camp. About 2,000 men were billeted in the town and surrounding district while a cluster of wooden huts were hurriedly assembled. For a time the billeting officer was former Newton Abbot urban councillor and taxi driver Bill Turpin.

The last occupants of the old Rawlinson Camp were members of the 47th Light Regiment, Royal Artillery, who used the base during their withdrawal from Aden. Before that it was home for many years to the Junior Leaders' Regiment, Royal Signals.

However, back in February 1970, nearest village Ogwell was on the warpath. But despite this reaction, the Home Office gave the thumbs-up to the prison plan that month. Massive opposition was expressed during a public meeting at Newton Abbot Racecourse in March and a full-scale inquiry was demanded from those who did not want prison inmates resident near their homes. In August 1970 Totnes MP Ray Mawby proposed Denbury Camp should become a touring caravan site rather than a prison.

But the prison project was given the all-clear in November, the Rural District Council subsequently objected and councillors demanded the plan be 'called in' for determination by the appropriate Government Minister. A holiday village was mooted for the site in December and Devon County Council called for an inquiry into the prison scheme. In January 1971 an agricultural use for the site was suggested and that holiday village, for 250 cottages, was proposed in March that year.

The long-anticipated public inquiry was held on 20 July at the racecourse and in January 1971 the 500-inmate jail was approved. In March the Home Office began scouring the Denbury area for 100 homes for prison staff.

In July 1972, a party of 350 men and women were given permission to train at the camp to prepare for a Commonwealth Expedition, known as Comex 5, led by the last commanding officer of the Junior Leaders' Regiment, Colonel Lionel Gregory – the man who founded the annual Ten Tors trek for youngsters on Dartmoor. The group, including Newton Grammar School teacher Sydney Williams, the man who organised the Christian Aid walks at the town racecourse each May, travelled 20,000 miles through India, Pakistan and South East Asia.

In September that year it was announced that Denbury Camp would be named Channings Wood Prison. Its first intake was on 1

May, 1974 and the establishment, with its eighty inmates, was officially opened twelve weeks later on 24 July by Dr Shirley Summerskill, Under Secretary of State at the Home Office, before some 200 guests.

She said that her department reported that constructing the place with inmate labour would save £2.5 million on the £6.3 million project. Concrete for the four large cell blocks, each to cater for a complement of 121, was cast at the prison and the inmates worked under supervision in groups of 43. Channings Wood had been declared Category C for prisoners deemed to have little or no wish to escape but needing some degree of security. Its first escape was on 21 October, 1974 and its first governor – Roy Clarke, outgoing deputy governor of Wormwood Scrubs (and not the chap who wrote *Last of the Summer Wine*) – bowed out in December 1976, when there were 500 prisoners billeted.

In December 1979 police began digging near the prison searching for the body of missing Army captain's wife Doris Symons who disappeared without trace 16 years earlier, allegedly murdered by her husband. Nothing was unearthed in the 20ft long tunnel gouged through ground at Ogwell Cross.

Capt Geoffrey Symons, who had died two years earlier, was posted to Rawlinson Barracks in March 1962. Doris, who he had married in 1947, vanished in 1971 and though there was no proof that she was dead the captain was charged with her murder. The sensational case became dubbed 'the no body murder.' Capt Symons claimed his wife had disappeared on a shopping trip to Plymouth, leaving behind her four-year-old son and all her possessions, and was acquitted on the final day of a one-week trial at Exeter Crown Court in February 1973. He spent 21 weeks in prison before his release and the case file, involving Scotland Yard, Interpol and the Australian police, was left open.

The 'Devil's' Faithful

On 13 June, 1970 hundreds of people, some in Quaker costume, walked into Bradley Wood and descended into a 60ft deep limestone basin – known as the 'Devil's Pit' – for a service commemorating a man and his followers who lived over 300 years earlier.

In 1662, under threat of fines, imprisonment or transportation, Revd William Yeo led a group of faithful non-conformists into the wood to worship, shielded by the dense undergrowth, tall trees and the darkness of night.

Newton Abbot Congregational Church and Plymouth Council for Churches members made the 1970 pilgrimage – thanks to more enlightened times, in daylight.

Feted Yachtsman

Round-the-world yachtsman Sir Alec Rose travelled to Newton Abbot Racecourse by motor launch for the town's third annual Trades Fair in June 1970. He had journeyed up the River Teign from Shaldon for the four-day event which featured more than fifty stalls and attracted 10,000 visitors.

A fruit merchant who developed a craving for single-handed sailing after World War Two, Sir Alec undertook a 155-day circumnavigation between July and December 1967 in his 36-foot converted cutter *Lively Lady*, travelling some 14,500 miles. After stops in Melbourne, Australia, and Bluff Harbour, New Zealand he arrived at Southsea the following July to cheering crowds, just ten days before his 60th birthday and was knighted the following day by the Queen.

He died in 1991 and is pictured (*right*) in his distinctive cap arriving at the racecourse.

Hustling on the Hustings

The late David Penhaligon, who many saw as the purveyor of honest good humour and common sense in politics, fought the Totnes Constituency against sitting MP Ray Mawby in June 1970, but came bottom of the poll in a three-cornered fight.

The ebullient Liberal had some consolation four years later, however, when he won the Truro seat. Brought up in the town and a former research and development engineer for Holman Brothers of Camborne, he was a cousin of actress Susan Penhaligon (*Bouquet of Barbed Wire*).

Totnes Conservative Mr Mawby – a former electrician who was nicknamed 'James Bond' in 1976, because his House of Commons pass had the same number as the world-famous fictional secret agent, 007 – was re-elected for the last time on 3 May, 1979 after a 24 year stint. He died in 1990.

Top Estate

The first 36 properties of the new Bradley Barton housing estate were completed in 1971, scooping a major award in the National House Building Council's scheme for the best homes of the decade as regional runners-up. The development grew rapidly, there was an energetic fight to get estate-based shops to cater for the expanding population and in 1979 Bradley Barton's own £250,000, 200-place primary school opened.

Bradley Mills, the Vicarys, Dyrons and the Penn Inn Pool

Bradley Mills closed on 12 February, 1971 after nearly two centuries of production, despite a £500,000 programme of alterations and extensions undertaken in the 1950s.

The building was owned by wool-combing firm John Vicary and Sons, which was established in Newton Abbot in 1747, though it originated in the Bideford and South Molton areas some years earlier. It was a paper mill in the early part of the century but this was destroyed in a fire and a new mill was built on the site in about 1860. This was also destroyed by fire and rebuilt in 1883.

Wool-processing machinery was first introduced at the start of World War One but a further fire in 1921 meant another rebuilding, after which the premises was equipped for wool-combing. It remained an independent tanning, fellmongery and wool-combing enterprise until 1939 when it became a subsidiary of Bradford company Sanderson, Murray and Elder Ltd.

Tanning was eventually discontinued because of difficulties in post-war trading but an expansion programme began in 1948. In the early 1950s synthetic fibre processing was introduced, at times taking the entire production capacity of the factory. When the end came the operation shrank severely and large-scale redundancies followed. Just before production finally stopped the workforce, which had numbered three hundred twenty years earlier, had dropped to just fifty.

In 1971 the former Vicary family home, Dyrons House, became a study and social centre for Sixth Form students at Newton Abbot Grammar School. The great stone building opposite the school site had a sweeping staircase, marble fireplaces, a large garden, Victorian conservatory and, up to a few weeks before the 4 March move, a private maze.

The Sixth Form had no centre before that. Pupils were stuffed into one small room at lunchtimes and their belongings stowed in corridor lockers. Private study was often undertaken in those same corridors, at the back of classrooms, and even in the toilets – whereas Dyrons House offered accommodation for 90 pupils.

Dyrons House, 1971

Devon County Council carried out major alterations and the students decorated most of the rooms. The parents association kicked off its relationship with the building by providing £100 for curtains and other items that would help remove any 'institutional feel' from the premises.

One reporter who visited the property that year wrote: "Once inside the house it is the retained elegance of the rooms that is imposing. Despite a rather hectic colour scheme on one of the top corridors, the décor, chosen by the warden Mr R.M. Perrin and applied enthusiastically by student volunteers, is generally not incongruous. Several of the fireplaces are particularly interesting, being art nouveau in character and adding an old-fashioned warmth to the new centrally-heated building."

On 1 July, 1995 Newton Abbot Sixth Form celebrated both its 25th anniversary and the centenary of Dyrons House. One of the guests was Robert Cook, headmaster at the time of the 1971 move.

The opening of the Dyrons Centre, 1975

Plans for the Dyrons Centre, on the adjoining site, were announced in September 1970 and its opening in 1975 brought comprehensive education to the town. The £677,000 complex provided 600 extra school places and included teaching rooms, a music, art and drama block, sports hall and youth centre. It was officially opened on 9 July, 1975 by education committee chairman Cllr Edward Day (*above*) and both Knowles Hill and Coombeshead schools relocated in September.

The £2.2 million 23-metre Teignbridge swimming pool opened on the site in 1989, replacing the former open air pool at Penn Inn which had served the town since its opening on 13 June, 1935 at a cost of nearly £7,000 to build.

Plans to improve Penn Inn's facilities were announced in December 1970. The cost of covering and upgrading the site was said to be £215,000 by January 1975. The popular bathing spot was never covered, despite a November 1979 petition to Teignbridge Council calling for the work to be done. Instead the pool was bulldozed and became home to a Plymco store in 1989, now Sainsbury's.

Newton Swimming Club members at a children's party in January 1973

Disk Sockey

The once-beloved disk jockey, *Jim'll Fix It* and *Top of the Pops* presenter Jimmy Savile, was besieged by Denbury villagers in March 1971 whilst on a Land's End to John O'Groats walk: they wanted him to open their upcoming fete. After all, TV's *Double Your Money* host Hughie Green had opened their 1970 event.

Unable to make the date, Savile – unveiled as a serial paedophile after his death – gave them a pair of his socks to raffle instead. I wonder who bought them – and what they paid...

Among the flood of stage, screen, sports and television faces visiting South Devon in the 1970s – either to open fetes, perform, or just relax between engagements – were tennis ace Sue Barker, Westward TV broadcaster Stuart Hutchinson, BBC news reader Richard Baker, 'Carry On' actor Sid James, comedian Harry Worth, pop group The Bachelors, singer Ivor Emmanual, entertainer Roy Hudd, cricket commentator Brian Johnston and singing duo Peters and Lee (Newton Abbot Woolworth's branch, 1979).

Of Hovercraft and Hydrofoils: Forde Park School

An establishment also to be tainted latterly by matters of child abuse, though long after it closed, was Forde Park School, eventually demolished for housing – though back in the 1970s this centre for 'problem boys' made news of a very different kind. For the lads helped build some pretty remarkable things during that decade – from the simple construction of bird boxes to the more elaborate go-karts for trials at Newton Abbot Racecourse. They also advertised their skills by manufacturing both a working hovercraft and a hydrofoil catamaran.

The two-seater hovercraft was so impressive that it went to the Toronto Trades Fair in 1970 and took second place in a national schools competition organised by British Petroleum before being bought by a Canadian firm. Sadly, their catamaran was less triumphant.

Pictured with the structural skeleton and plans for the hydrofoil in May 1972: its inventor Christopher Hook and school engineering master Brian Holmes

The school constructed their hydrofoil catamaran *Miss Strand Glass III* in May 1972 in an attempt to break the world speed sailing record, then at 29.3 knots (33mph). The vessel was ready for testing by July but failed in October. Though hitting 14.17 knots in her attempts at the record in Weymouth in September 1974, *Miss Strand Glass III* unfortunately broke a mast and lost one of its foils to a mooring.

The original Newton College was established in Courtenay Road in 1861 and moved to the College Road site in 1864, extending over the next two decades. In 1940 it amalgamated with Kelly College, Tavistock. The Home Office created a junior approved school on the site, starting with 101 boys and ten staff which was modernised in the mid-1960s. In 1972 the school lost its Home Office ties to become a community home with education under Devon's social services department, licensed to take seventy boys aged from ten to fourteen. The adjoining Milton House was bought as an annex.

Its curriculum included sailing, mountaineering, cooking, judo, orienteering and adventure weekends as well as traditional school subjects. This is when the workshops became active, building the go-karts, the hovercraft and hydrofoil.

By 1983 the number of boys at the school had dropped to thirty and plans were made to change the 'community home for problem boys' into a child care centre. This fell through and the school closed on 31 July, 1985 with just four boys remaining – and then the buildings went up for auction.

In December 1985, 425 lots went to 160 purchasers including a three-quarters size snooker table sold for £1,000. In March 1985 the 15-acre playing fields below the school, between Coach Road and Decoy Park, were bought by Teignbridge Council with an offer of £70,000. Suggestions that the old school swimming pool on the site could replace the Penn Inn pool were abandoned due to cost.

In May, the one-and-a-half acre site at Church Road that housed the former staff accommodation of Milton House and Milton Court – the latter a brace of semi-detached houses – was sold at auction for £293,000. Another staff building, Trevanion, at 10 College Road, went at the same session for £67,000. The four-acre school site was sold at auction for £730,000 to Barratts in July 1987 and was subsequently redeveloped with housing.

Just One Pint Today, Please…

One of Britain's last cycling milkmen, Charles Stow, made his final

Newton Abbot rounds in early October, 1970 before hanging up his bottles for the last time.

Over 45 years he carried around 40 pints daily in crates perched in his sturdy carry basket and covering a twenty mile route from Mile End and Broadlands to Milber and Buckland delivering both milk and cream to local doorsteps, sourced from Milber Dairies. Aged 63, Torquay United fan Mr Stow had decided to call it a day due to his wife's ill health and his round was taken over by Devonshire Dairies.

He is pictured loaded and ready to deliver, toting a consignment of 42 pints: that's nearly 53 lbs, or 19 kgs, or eight stone, which is heavier than a beer keg (and nearly the weight of an adult octopus, even though you didn't ask) – which is an extraordinary load to propel up and down hills on a bicycle!

✂ Snippets #1
He's Got Legs

When Cottle and Austen's Circus came to town in August 1971, cyclist Raymond Darke, of Highweek, found himself lost under the legs of a promotional stilt walker outside Liptons in Courtenay Street. No-one was hurt…

Meter Moo

Shoppers were taken aback in December 1971 to see a parking meter close to the market. They were even more surprised to see that it had a live calf tethered to it. But it turned out that there was nothing sinister afoot: both animal and machine had been imported as props for a television commercial.

Solid Gold Smile

Miss World Belinda Green paid a visit to Newton Abbot in April 1973 as part of a whistle-stop West Country tour. The 20-year-old from Sydney, Australia was promoting and signing copies of Windmill Records' LP *Miss World's Solid Gold Top Twenty*, which featured artists such as Roxy Music and T Rex. She did not perform on any of the tracks. [Windmill's *Parade of Pops* titles were one of the longest-running cover tunes series, with 26 regular installments to their credit, going into 1976 when the series was finally shelved.]

Dingles

The House of Fraser took over Dingles in Courtenay Street in 1972. Originally Badcocks of Newton Abbot, the premises was sold to Dingles in 1969. The Dingles store closed in 1988, the building was demolished in 1993 and it was rebuilt with a mock Edwardian façade to house a new Boots branch in 1994.

Odeon Cinema

The 1930s Odeon Cinema was bought by motor garage Seymour Horwell in June 1972 and ceased showing films. The leasehold of the site was acquired by Teignbridge Council in 1978 and the premises were subsequently demolished. The Odeon opened on 17 February, 1936 and staff celebrated its 21st anniversary in 1957 along with manager Leslie Crossland and chief projectionist S.S. Sarahs who had both served the popular picture house from the outset

A snap of the clock tower taken from a window of the soon-to-be-gone Odeon Cinema. Just visible, part-way up Courtenay Street behind the white van is the frontage of the old Wesleyan Methodist Church, demolished in the 1960s, its spire removed for safety reasons in the early 1900s. The old power station chimneys rise from the horizon.

Sandford Orleigh – and the lady who was nearly a slave

Rumours that unoccupied historic Regency mansion Sandford Orleigh was due to be sold began circulating in June 1972. Its Exeter Road location, with panoramic views of the Teign Estuary, Haldon Hills and Dartmoor, is recorded in the Domesday Book and the property was once home to the Templer family, and later renowned explorer Sir Samuel White Baker. It had been used as a hotel following World War Two and became a private school in 1959; it had gained a Grade II listing in 1949, but had been empty for some time in the Seventies, suffering from weather damage and vandalism.

Its new owner, Newton Abbot property developer Brian Caunter, unsuccessfully applied to demolish the listed building and redevelop the site with housing – a proposal that caused an outcry at both local and national levels due to the land's historical significance. Even after he sold the property to school principal Melvin Denton his company A.C. Young planned to develop the 23,000 sq ft mansion into a restaurant complex. But the 1975 scheme came to nothing and the building was renovated for Lupton House lower school.

Taking children from seven to eleven with behavioral difficulties, the school opened on 13 January, 1976, but finally closed in June 1990 and the place was put back on the market for £50,000. It was sold in 1992 to a Plymouth buyer who apparently planned to turn it into a Christian centre. But this did not materialize and in 1993 Teignbridge Council called for urgent renovation works as the building was in a poor state. It was later renovated and converted into apartments.

The manor was built in 1830 on the foundations of a much older house by prominent Georgian industrialist George Templer. Templer built the eight-mile granite tramway from Haytor to Kingsteignton to link with the Stover Canal, previously excavated by his father James to transport ball clay mined in the area to Teignmouth for export.

The forty-roomed house was later home to Samuel White Baker, known as 'Baker Pasha,' from November 1874 until his death in December 1893. His widow remained at Sandford Orleigh until her death, heirless, in March 1916.

She was his second wife (Baker's first wife having died in 1854) and he first set eyes on her when she was being offered for sale in a Turkish market. Baker outbid a Turk for the 17-year-old Hungarian refugee, Florence Barbara Mary Finnian von Sass, and she subsequently followed him in his adventures for five years – including exploring the upper reaches of the Nile where he discovered and named the Murchison Falls and Lake Albert Nyanza.

The couple were secretly married in London in 1865 and when Queen Victoria knighted her husband later that year Miss von Sass became Lady Florence Baker.

But how did Sandford Orleigh get its name?

In 1996 the granddaughter of Sir Samuel's head gardener Albert Willis explained that her late father Walter, a Royal Navy engine room artificer, told her that *Sandford Orleigh* was a combination of the names of two of Albert's employer's gardeners. Sir Samuel favoured calling the house Sandford – but what of Sandford's fellow gardener Leigh? Then Lady Baker suggested combining the two names, and the linked 'Sandford Or Leigh' was born. Mr Willis heard the story from a Kingsteignton friend who studied local estates and their histories.

Mr Willis's granddaughter Mrs Betty Matthews produced archive photographs of the interior of the mansion when the Bakers were in residence and these were published on 12 April, 1996 in the *Mid-Devon Advertiser*. They show the billiard room, that later became the school dining room, with its animal heads and skins, and the drawing room crammed with trophies and exotic Victoriana.

The billiard room in the Baker-era Sandford Orleigh

The drawing room of Sandford Orleigh

A huge and striking carved oak overmantle that dominated one of the main rooms of the mansion was donated to the town museum in 2008 and now has pride of place at the far end of its new premises at Newton's Place, Wolborough Street, displayed below the original stained glass windows of the former St Leonard's Church.

The converted grade two listed building became an antiques centre after church use from 1836 to 1997 ceased and was empty and deteriorating for many years before Newton Abbot Town Council bought the building and embarked on a £2 million project, supported by local and national funding, including the Heritage Lottery Fund, to reclaim it as a museum, town hall and community space.

The mainly 16th-century overmantle is a Tudor period reredos carved in the then-fashionable Renaissance style of *all'antica* ('in the style of antiquity'), its earliest sources taken from trees felled in 1517. A meticulous restoration of the piece, which resembles a screen in Bradley Manor and the south door of Totnes Church, was undertaken by Hugh Harrison Conservation.

Furled

A unique building specialising in umbrella making and recovering as well as the repair of trunks, Langford's, closed in April, 1972. C. Langford & Co was established in Queen Street in 1879 (the date of our picture below). It moved to Courtenay Street and was eventually purchased by Devon County Council for demolition as part of redevelopment plans. Mr C. Langford, chief shareholder and son of the founder, said at the time: "The art of umbrella repairing is fast dying out. It will be a sad day when we close the shop." And it was.

Another victim of the changing times was late Victorian men's outfitters Laws and Wareham that closed on 2 June, 1979 after over a century of trading in the town, the shop facing Lloyds Bank. The business was founded in 1860 by Frank W. Law who later went into partnership with George Wareham. At one time the business employed thirty people, including six tailors.

New Stations

Newton Abbot's £50,000 replacement fire and ambulance stations at Balls Corner were officially opened on 13 November, 1972 by urban council chairman Cllr Frances Humpherson. Previously they had operated from what was termed 'a little shed' in Market Street.

The complex was the first in the county to have a 'quick getaway' system whereby traffic lights on the road outside were controlled from inside the station. Difficulties with the foundations had briefly delayed completion.

Excuse me, Ma'am

Newton Abbot's war memorial at Devon Square, on the junction between Queen Street and The Avenue, received a 50th birthday sprucing up from council workmen William Bailey and William Stephens in October 1972.

The monument was unveiled in 1922 in the presence of Lieutenant General Sir Charles Louis Woollcombe, KCB, KCMG. It was designed by Coleridge D. White and sculpted by E.M. Courtenay Pollock and commemorates both the First and Second World Wars, as well as further campaigns in Korea, Iraq and Afghanistan and the Malayan Emergency. A large oak tree was felled to make way for it despite public objections.

What's in a Name – Lemon?

The prime player in the flooding of Newton Abbot, and particularly the fateful 1979* episode (along with the adverse weather and the tides, of course) was the River Lemon: just a small, 16km stretch of water linking the slopes of Dartmoor with the Teign Estuary.

Rising in hills east of Widecombe, the watercourse runs under the town centre along a narrow stone channel, and whilst vessels used to load and unload as far upstream as the recently-resurrected town quay, and even further inland in earlier times, no sea-going craft has ventured past the Shaldon Bridge for many decades.

Yet the Lemon's name is a subject for debate. According to researcher Felicity McCulloch: "At the time of King John the river was known as *Limonstream*, in description of the limestone rocks rising steeply on either bank, or alternatively originates from the Celtic word for *elm*, or could stem from the Saxon word *llammau*, being drawn from the stone boulders lying on the river bed whose literal meaning is 'stones in a river to walk upon.'"

It has also been suggested that the name may have come from the Greek word for port or harbour, *limani* (Λιμάνι).

This is not implausible, as the custodians of religion, medicine, science and the legal profession all used both Greek and Latin extensively in mediaeval times (less exclusively now) – as would have the Abbots of Torre who not only had command of a substantial acreage of Newton Abbot but would have participated in the extensive trading that took place at Newton town, its busy Quay, Hackney (latterly shipping china clay) and along the River Teign.

One thing is certain, though – we definitely are not known for growing lemons in South Devon!

(*See page 104)

'Tiny'

Still a familiar sight on the down platform of Newton Abbot railway station in the 1970s was the only-surviving broad-gauge locomotive, Tiny, build in 1868 and used for shunting and later for operating pumps at the boiler house, hence being nicknamed 'The Coffee Pot.'

She stood on a 7ft length of track and was much-admired by passengers arriving or embarking before being retired in 1980 to the South Devon railway museum at Buckfastleigh.

Streaking down for half a pint

WITH a flash of flesh, and a hearty "Hi ho, Streaker!", the Borough of Penryn was assailed on Saturday evening by the latest American craze —streaking.

There were two men involved. One raced into a fish and chip shop in West Street and asked for a meal. The shop was empty at the time. The proprietor, Mr. MacCartney, said: "I thought he was mad." He did not notice that his customer was totally nude until he was leaving the shop.

'NO PANIC'

"There was no panic," he said, "I didn't see anyone running after him."

The second man visited The Three Tuns. The landlord, Mr. G. R. K. Bolitho, said that the man ordered a half-pint of beer and then left.

The pub was quite full at the time, but the customers treated the incident with amusement. The streaker was naked, except for a piece of string tied round his ankle. No doubt to remind him to put his clothes back on!

The whole thing was purported to have started as a bet.

> One of those periodically popular pastimes of the 1970s was the gentle art of streaking where ordinary people shed their clothes and cantered (or strolled) through public areas divested of their customary decorum, to a combination of laughter and embarrassment. Though nothing to do with Newton Abbot – or, indeed, Devon – this piece is one of my favourites from the time, courtesy of the *Falmouth Packet*, so I hope that readers will indulge me for one page.

No Power for the People

The cooling tower falls

One of the major structures that had dominated the town skyline from most directions for nearly five decades – Newton Abbot power station – was finally dispatched in the nineteen seventies.

The decision to close this important operation with the loss of forty jobs took place against a background of industrial unrest and a three-day week and was announced in February 1973 to strong urban council opposition. Some of the older plant had already been demolished in 1972, reducing the station's capacity from 55,500 kilowatts to 37,500 kW. Initially the Central Electricity Generating Board talked of building a gas turbine plant as a replacement, but this came to nothing.

The great red-brick building, more than 100ft tall with its companion 250ft cooling tower, was mothballed – a decision severely criticised by urban councillors who called for its reinstatement. They could not understand why one of Britain's most efficient stations should be gathering cobwebs instead of generating power, surrounded by 18,000 tons of valuable coal. They seethed at the thought of that coal being transported from Newton Abbot to another station in East Yelland – at an estimated cost of £3 per ton – when local men were 'ready and able' to generate enough electricity to serve 100,000 homes. A deputation to London to see CEGB chairman Arthur Hopkins produced no change.

Just before demolition began in earnest a new home was sought for the power station's resident cat Sooty, who was fourteen, had lived there for almost all of her life and had produced about sixty kittens along the way. (*See photo next page*).

The station's closing down ceremony was held in March 1974 and a plaque commemorating its opening nearly fifty years earlier, in September 1924, was presented to urban council chairman Cllr Mrs Frances Humpherson, to be placed among the council's mementoes for display on appropriate occasions. She is pictured with the plaque and (*left to right*) Norman Finch, station superintendent of Plymouth and Newton Abbot; Ken Nicholls, deputy superintendent, Newton Abbot; and Donald Pask, director general of the CEGB South West region.

The cooling tower was finally felled on Sunday, 8 September 1974. Holes had been drilled in the tower's shell to take the 46 lbs of explosives and 220,000 tons of reinforced concrete was collapsed from the bottom, angled slightly towards the adjacent station building. That main building was finally demolished at the end of 1977 and during the operation a teenage worker died when he fell from the roof. The whole site has since been developed with housing.

Sooty, with maintenance engineer Harry Harwood – and Cllr Mrs Humpherson with the close-down plaque

Power station portrait

View from the power station roof, just prior to its demolition, looking towards Newton Road and showing the line of the river, railway sidings, the old garages, former Advertiser hut and white SWEB building in Wharf Road; the Balls Corner junction is upper left below the hill

The power station, viewed up river across Hackney Marshes from the Passage House Inn in 1972

Keep Our Casualty Unit!

Newton Abbot Hospital's casualty department reopened after an acrimonious six-month closure in January 1973, and its local need was immediately demonstrated when it catered for some eighty patients during its first week.

A nationwide shortage of casualty officers was the reason given in March 1971 for its closure. But Newtonians put up a strong protest at the switch to Torbay Hospital and a Round Table petition calling for the service to return to Newton was signed by 13,000 people.

The idea for a hospital for the town was first raised at a Town Hall meeting on 20 May, 1873 and a house in East Street was bought for the purpose for £750, just below the Baptist Chapel and accommodating thirteen patients. Torquay Water Corporation agreed to supply the premises with mains water for one shilling per year. A larger unit further up the hill was eventually opened on a site donated by a Mr Scratton, 'Squire of the Ogwells,' and a Mrs Fisher paid £6,000 to create the first part of the new building as a memorial to her late husband. It was run on a voluntary basis until 1948, though the designation Cottage Hospital had been dropped in 1899 when a porter's lodge and gateway were added.

It was first enlarged in the late 1920s, the foundation stone for the new wing being laid by Lord Mildmay of Fleet with the official opening being undertaken by HRH Edward, Prince of Wales, in 1927. According to columnist Edith Wheeler, writing in a 21 March, 1970 article on the history of the town hospital and recalling that occasion, "the Prince arrived in by no means a good temper."

The reason for this, she said, was that "he had just come from Exeter where the citizens of that ever-loyal city had shown their enthusiasm by shaking his hand so violently that it became extremely painful. When he arrived at Newton Abbot the streets were lined with schoolchildren eager to give their Prince a great big welcome, but all they saw was a closed car speeding up to the hospital."

In January 1971 only three of twelve Newton Abbot General Practitioners supported a health centre for the town, and in September 1976 doctors also opposed plans for a new maternity unit at Torbay Hospital, wanting the service to stay in Newton Abbot. In both cases their opinions were superseded and in 2009 the East Street hospital closed and its replacement is now based in premises on West Golds Road, Jetty Marsh, operating a wide range of services but with no on-site outpatients' department.

Part of hospital is 'health and safety hazard!'

THE Physiotherapy Department of Newton Abbot Hospital has been dubbed a health and safety hazard.

The criticism was made in the report of a five-strong visiting panel of Torbay District Community Health Council.

The panel complained that the department is:

- Housed in a 32-year old Nissen hut, bought for £75 in 1947 when it was scheduled to house the department for just two years.
- Cluttered up with good equipment in the gymnasium area.
- Virtually without storage accommodation, and cardboard boxes are perched on anything that will hold them.
- Without an internal toilet.

The report said that two fire doors 'were hardly approachable because of fitted equipment like exercising bars'. The office was

Department crammed into old £75 hut

tiny and the staff-room 'microscopic'.

Extension

If patients needed to go to the toilet they had to re-dress and go outside to use a public toilet. The staff toilet, also outside, was 'anything but perfect'.

'The panel was particularly distressed and concerned about this department,' said Mrs A. Jenkins in the report. 'There was no doubt about it being a health and safety hazard.'

The department operated on part-time staff, 'but working conditions such as those offered would not attract new, energetic, career-minded young people.'

Waiting

The panel concluded that a plan to build an extension to the department, at a cost of £13,000, would be 'inappropriate and wasteful.'

It urged: 'The whole department needs re-building. Room seems to be available for this purpose, for a re-constructed unit could be built on the present site with, if necessary, additional land which is at the moment waste land.'

Though accepting that the general part of the hospital was 'sparkling clean, fresh and well-decorated,' the panel felt that it 'did not seem fully utilised — and in view of the fact that 'there were waiting lists at Newton Abbot, the panel wondered why.

'Perhaps it was because of shortage of staff?'

Horrified

The panel was 'horrified' to learn that there were only three members of staff on duty at night, with a fourth member acting as a 'runner'.

The report was considered at last week's meeting of the health council, which will discuss it further when the District Management Team submits some plans of the hospital.

Cutting from 1979...

The Family Department Store

Austins, 1935, celebrating the Silver Jubilee of King George V

Newton Abbot department store Austins celebrated its 50th anniversary on 20 March, 1973. The family-owned business was founded on 1 March, 1923 when Robert Austin bought the small Courtenay Street premises of draper W.T. White. Mr Austin, from Romford in Essex, remained active as head of the company until his death in 1950, shortly after his 81st birthday. He was succeeded by his son Charles Austin whose son David currently runs the expanded business.

A new extension was opened in November 1978 and a further expansion took place in 1993 into the former Globe Hotel – once an important posting house and often referred to as 'the jewel in the town' that closed in 2000. The store now has a separate furniture department and a fourth unit comprising a menswear outlet and a remarkable toy shop that attracts customers from all over the region.

(Also see *The Spin of the Globe,* page 69).

Poles Apart

Ilford Park Polish Home at Stover finally got central heating in its former army hut accommodations in 1973 and in 1977 the *Advertiser* published a major feature on the unique complex, created at the end of World War Two to house those Polish nationals under British command who wanted to stay in Britain at the end of hostilities.

'Little Poland,' as it was known, with its original 950 ex-servicemen, their families and dependents, was one of 42 'camps' – they naturally preferred the word 'community' – and in 1968 it became the last of its kind with 276 elderly residents, many disabled.

They were accommodated in wooden huts built to quarter American troops based around Heathfield before the D-Day landings. Rumours still persist – backed-up by various tell-tale finds over the years – that the Americans buried tons of military hardware in the area before they returned home after the war. These discarded items included trucks, jeeps and munitions. A US naval stores depot was based at Heathfield in the 1940s and troops trained on Bovey Heath.

In 1977 the Polish community comprised a 180-seater Catholic Church with pine pews brought from London and renovated locally, a 2,000-volume library, general stores, 342 individual rooms, a staff of 77 and 30 hospital personnel. Residents were regularly entertained by the 35-strong Malwy group of Polish dancers; some residents tended their own gardens and others made cushion covers, table cloths, napkins and rugs for sale.

In 1992 a £6.2 million state-of-the-art replacement home was opened for the remaining residents on the large site set next to Stover Golf Club. Lord Henley laid the foundation stone and formally opened the home in December at a ceremony attended by the Polish Consul General, representatives of Polish organisations and the then DSS Permanent Secretary. The new premises provided an 81-bed residential care wing, 14-bed nursing home and three bungalows.

A Towering Pageant

Newtonians turned out in their hundreds to celebrate their most famous monument, St Leonard's Tower, in June 1973. It was, after all, the residents who had fended off demolition in 1897 by voting in a town council poll to keep the ancient church tower where it was, in the centre of a junction of four roads in Courtenay Street.

Five days of events, culminating in a mediaeval pageant and mammoth procession, was held from 12-16 June, 1973, also celebrating the completion of a major restoration programme. The tower had been conveyed from Wolborough Parochial Church Council on 16 December, 1971 for its care and maintenance. The 1973 scheme involved a new roof, floors, access stairway, new steel bell frame, renovation of bells and clock (converting to electric winding), cleaning and re-pointing the stonework and providing seating, electric lights and heating.

The project had been largely due to the persistence of Cllr Arthur Shobbrook, who had declared that the tower was the 'landmark of the town' and should not be allowed to deteriorate. A commemorative plaque was unveiled by Cllr Shobbrook, who died in January 1970 and never saw the result of his championing.

More than twenty floats took part in a parade led on horseback by Roger Warren, as William of Orange, followed in a blue Rolls-Royce by UDC chairman Cllr Mrs Frances Humpherson and the Bishop of Crediton who later conducted a service of re-dedication for the tower. The festivities included mummers, dancers, acrobats, a ram roast, a ducking stool, puppet show, Maypole dancing, hand bell ringing, mediaeval jousting and country sports.

Two Chinese canons, formerly displayed in Courtenay Park, were unveiled at the tower in February 1976 by Town Mayor Cllr David Prouse. It was Cllr Prouse who had wryly suggested in February

1973 that the historic building be sold to America, engendering howls of protest. The gun carriages were replaced in 1990 and in November 1979 Newton transport firm Snells Coaches added a St Leonard's Tower motif to their livery.

The chapel part of the tower, thought to date back to 1220, was demolished in 1836, leaving the tower standing alone at the busy road junction (now a pedestrianised area) and poised to become the subject of innumerable postcards. A clock was added in 1874.

The celebratory procession of 1973 winds its way up Courtenay Street towards the tower. The Globe Hotel is pictured front left with Austins department store to the right

New Council – Ancient House

A new local authority configuration kicked into gear at the start of the financial year in 1974. The changes were being planned in April 1971, aiming to reduce the size of local government by doing away with its urban and rural tiers and creating larger 'district' authority catchments.

The first chief executive for the replacement council, based in Newton Abbot and on old 'Teignbridge' district boundaries, was solicitor Eric Loveys, appointed in July 1973 along with a group of members from the outgoing councils who would guide the new set-up until at least its first public elections. The last rites for Newton Abbot Rural District Council were held in April 1974 as the new authority took over and Teignbridge District Council was birthed.

Of this inaugural group, several were still Teignbridge councillors after local government elections in 1975 including Cllrs Fernley Holmes (Bovey Tracey), Leslie Pike (Whitestone), Horace Hawkins (Haytor), Mrs Di Nicholls and David Prouse (both Newton Abbot).

The TDC steering committee, posing at the racecourse in June, 1973

The fledgling authority moved into the old Newton Abbot RDC offices in Kingsteignton Road, opened in January 1937 and built for £6,400, latterly home to county social services offices and now rebuilt as flats. It was inadequate accommodation, with a proliferation of scattered huts being used as offices.

The council acquired its own armorial bearings and in December 1976 set its sights on the old Odeon Cinema as a possible new home. This did not work out and in January 1978 members decided to bid for the historic Forde House, owned by the Sellick family since 1960 and housing Forde House Antiques at the time.

In February members agreed in less than ten seconds to buy the property and the historic Grade I listed Elizabethan mansion and its eleven acres of grounds changed hands for £62,000. Its acquisition was all the council needed as a fillip to creating its own complex, but a considerable amount of money had first to be spent on renovating the ageing building, including extensive (and expensive) roof repairs.

In 1984 work started on erecting a new headquarters behind Forde House and the £3 million scheme was completed in 1987, providing a centre for the entire council operation which had previously been spread across a number of separate, far-flung buildings.

The Passmore Edwards Ownership Tussle

A long-running dispute between Newton Abbot Town Council and Devon County Council over ownership of the town's striking Passmore Edwards building erupted in 1974.

Town councillors laid claim to the premises, housing the public library, saying it should have passed to them in the carve-up of civic assets that took place on local government reorganisation in 1973, especially as the building was owned by the outgoing urban council up to the change-over.

Never able to find sufficient documentation to support its case and unwilling to go to the public expense of fighting the issue in the High Court the town council eventually dropped the matter, but not before six years of wrangling, abuse, petitions, claim and counter-claim, sudden clues and dead ends.

Finally, the town council accepted a county option to buy the building, over the following eighty years, should the library use ever cease (to date, it hasn't). A price would be assessed if the situation ever arose and the county added that it might consider aiding that purchase.

Both the library and the associated technical school (an addition largely attributable to a proposal by Charles and William Vicary) were opened with silver keys on 18 August, 1904. Confetti sellers apparently did a roaring trade as Market Street was reportedly carpeted with the stuff. The Lord Lieutenant of Devon, Lord Ebrington, launched the Free Library and Lord Clifford of Chudleigh opened the school.

The distinctive building, in worked limestone with terracotta dressing, was given to the town by West Country philanthropist Passmore Edwards, whose mother was born in a house in Wolborough Street. The site was paid for by public subscription.

In July 1975 – ousted from its previous home in Courtenay Street by the demands of the market redevelopment and forced to use cramped offices in Sherborne Road for administration duties and committee meetings and the library's reference rooms for full council sessions – the town council decided to buy the Berwyn Hotel in East Street for a 'town home.' But a public meeting rejected the idea with a 30-22 vote in July and in August the council began looking at architect Jeremy Newcombe's former premises at 2 St Paul's Road for a potential town hall.

The place had been home to railways engineer Isambard Kingdom Brunel during building works on Great Western's Newton Abbot to Torquay and Newton to Plymouth lines and the council moved there in 1978 with an official opening on 20 January. In November that year the town council considered twinning with German town Besigheim and the charter was officially signed in Sepember 1979.

Members discussed buying 2 St Paul's Road two months later, but instead moved next door to the larger and former YMCA building at 9 Devon Square, renaming it Great Western House in a deal largely financed by the sale of some council land earmarked for redevelopment as flats. The council's new home generously accommodated the council chamber and offices as well as a railway museum including working signals from the town's downgraded railway station.

Five Mayors served the town between 1974, when the town council was re-constituted, and 1979; consecutively Cllrs Edgar Hewett (a former local railwayman), David Prouse, Vince Bartlett (also a former town railwayman), Alan Forster, Mrs Frances Humpherson and Mrs Nancy Morrison.

Is There a Doctor in the House?

In October 1974, a BBC film crew visited Dartmoor to film sequences for *The Sontaran Experiment*, a two-part *Dr Who* adventure written by Bob Baker and Dave Martin and screened on 22 February and 1 March, 1975.

During filming, Tom Baker slipped and broke his collarbone. According to fan sites, producer Philip Hinchcliffe thought the injury so serious that he might have to re-cast the newly-appointed actor, so he had designer Roger Murray-Leach drive the injured party to the nearest hospital.

Hinchcliffe was relieved when the injury turned out to be much less serious and Baker was able and willing to continue filming the next day. The lengthy coloured scarf the Doctor customarily wore covered an unsightly neck brace, but fight arranger Terry Walsh still ended up doubling for the future star in several shots.

The two-parter was shot entirely on location and on videotape and the episodes also involved Elisabeth Sladen (Sarah Jane Smith), Kevin Lindsay (Sontaran Field Major Styre) and Peter Rutherford (Roth).

(Pictures next page)

Tom Baker was the longest-serving actor to portray the Doctor – for seven seasons from 1974 to 1981, a total of 172 episodes.

Fortuitously, *Advertiser* photographer Arthur Kay was on hand to take the pictures in Baker's opening year.

Old Town Hall, But New Courthouse

The original glass doors to the town council's council chamber; plus the former town hall, magistrates' and county court frontage in Queen Street, demolished as part of the Market Walk redevelopment

The problem with rainwater leaks in Newton Abbot's post-war courthouse – the former Town Hall in Courtenay Street – was condemned as 'disgraceful' in January 1975.

It was generally regarded as a court with dreadful acoustics, prompting cupped palms clapped around ears and murmurs of "What did he say?" during magistrates' hearings

Dusty netting strung loosely across the ceiling did little to help with sound-proofing the cavernous room with its old and uncomfortable pew-styled wooden seating.

In February 1976 it was announced that the place was to close – to be removed as part of the centre redevelopment – and a new £250,750 court house would be built in Newfoundland Way, conveniently just below the town police station.

The notable glass doors to the ground floor chambers, inscribed with the town crest, were earmarked by the town council and provided the entrance to the first floor council chamber in their new town hall, Great Western House.

The court spent two years operating from Teignmouth, from May 1976 to its first sitting in its Newfoundland Way premises on 3 October, 1978. In July 1977, chairman of the magistrates Cllr Leonard Lamb buried a magistrate's handbook, court list and other official documents in a sealed box in the brickwork of the partly-constructed shell, looking to the future when it would be torn down. It was hoped a later generation would find the contents of interest.

The complex was officially opened by the Lord Chancellor, Lord Elwyn-Jones on 20 September, a market day, a decision that caused some discontent. Traders complained that one hundred much-needed market day parking spaces had been lost to official visitors. The Odeon car park was closed all day and 24 spaces in the Newfoundland Way car park were also taken up.

When requested, the Lord Chancellor told Powderham Road residents that he could not help them in their pressing fight for a pedestrian crossing in East Street. And MP Ray Mawby was cross because he did not get an invitation to the ceremony – normal practice when a government minister visits an MP's constituency. A spokesman for the Devon Magistrates' Court Committee responded rather insensitively that there had been limited space available and "if Mr Mawby had been invited it would not have stopped there."

✂ Snippets #2
Go-Go Went-Went

In May 1974 it was announced that topless go-go dancing sessions at the Jolly Sailor public house in East Street at lunchtimes each Wednesday and Sunday were to end, as the landlord thought his clients were growing tired of them. However, they continued and during the summer employers began to complain that their workmen were returning late from lunch on Wednesdays because of the distraction. It took local magistrates, ruling against the activity in February 1975, to finally stop it. The licensee then closed the pub and left the town, apparently without telling the brewery which then sought re-possession of the premises. After being closed for some months the pub was reopened as the Jolly Abbot in 1976 under new management – but sans lunchtime cavorting.

Marsh Road Sports Centre

The £47,000 Newton Abbot Recreational Trust premises was formally opened on 18 September, 1971 providing facilities for football, cricket and hockey. The pavilion was earmarked for Newton Spurs, Newton 66 Soccer Club, South Devon Cricket Club and the trust's own tennis and squash clubs. The four tennis courts were opened in April 1973 by former British number one Mike Sangster. The new sports centre in Marsh Road was given the green light by the UDC in March 1970 after four hours of talks. Work began in October and the foundation stone was laid on 13 February, 1971 by Trust president Arthur Morgan.

Menzies Closes

Newsagent John Menzies closed its Courtenay Street shop on 15 March, 1975 after twelve years on the same site and a 1968 face-lift. Part of the reason for dropping its retail outlet in the town was due to rival newsagent W.H. Smiths transferring its Queen Street premises to Courtenay Street in October the previous year. The Menzies property was subsequently bought by American-owned jewellery firm Zales.

Five-Figure Centre

Buckland and Milber community centre was opened on 12 April, 1975. It cost around £60,000 to build and the rising cost of the project had been the subject of some controversy since 1973.

Chamber Lady

As if to herald coming times, Newton Abbot Chamber of Trade elected its first lady to the chair in February 1978. Betty Solon, a partner in the firm Craftsmen Cleaners Ltd, took over from retiring chairman Alan Baker.

The Spin of the Globe

The two-star Globe Hotel, with its 22 bedrooms, two bars and two restaurants, was put on the market in April 1975 when it was 138 years old.

The property was taken over by London-based Janorvale Ltd but in September 1979 a receiver-manager was appointed by the mortgagees to put the place back on a sound financial footing. Janorvale started High Court proceedings against the decision, but was itself compulsorily wound up in April 1980 and the premises came into the hands of the Official Receiver. The bars and restaurants continued to trade throughout its troubled year, though the hotel side was closed.

In December 1980 the Mogford family, who ran the Highweek Inn, bought The Globe and re-opened the hotel. But the place finally closed completely in 1988 and remained empty until the building was converted into three shops. It was acquired by Austins in 1992 and remodelled into an extension of its original store, across the road in Courtenay Street, to coincide with the store's 70th anniversary year in 1993.

Donkeys' Ears

Brief rural lanes digression: A previously-unpublished seventies study of snow and winter donkeys. Say Awwww (or Haaaaw)…

A Priest's House – or Not – and the Squandered Stones

In April 1975 a 13th-century building known as the Priest's House was demolished in Highweek Street to make way for a road-widening scheme which also saw the demise of the less-historic adjoining VacServices premises. Three years later, the Seven Stars pub was also demolished, pulling its last pint on 31 July, 1978.

At the time, Newton Abbot historian Trixie Lamb – wife of magistrate and councillor Leonard – fought strenuously to have the dilapidated but listed building retained and collected a 1,190-signature petition to *Save the House*.

The Priest's House, extreme right

But the property was flattened and the 124 stones of the front wall were said to have been numbered and stored at Teignbridge Council's Forde Road depot. The site was cleared for an archaeological dig in December when members of the Devon Committee for Rescue Archaeology uncovered a floor level estimated to be 17th-century.

Just before the dig was terminated in August 1976, archaeologists revealed that Highweek Street had been raised by three or four feet in the 17th-century to avoid flooding from the nearby River Lemon. However, they had come across no evidence that the building had any religious connection, though it was clearly once the home of a man of means.

The Priest's House archaeological dig, 1976

During the market square redevelopment it was suggested by some councillors that the Priest's House facade could be rebuilt as a feature in the new shopping centre. This failed to materialise but, in July 1984, district policy committee members said the bricks should return to Highweek Street as part of that redevelopment, with the contractor footing the bill.

In January 1991 open-mouthed Teignbridge councillors were told that over half of the stored stones had been used for a sewerage scheme, to build the head wall of a culvert – and what was left of the old house frontage, about fifty stones, was unsuitable for either rebuilding or using in further engineering schemes. The remainder would be offered to the town museum.

At least one stone, however, returned to Highweek Street. It was placed in the gable end of the St Mary's Court sheltered housing development, completed in 1992.

Local Publishers Hit "Rocky Patch"

For specialist publishing company David & Charles, 1975 was a bad year.

A downturn in the national economy forced it out of its spacious two floor headquarters over the booking office at Newton Abbot's railway station and into new premises in Brunel Road.

The home they had to quit was built, along with the main line station, in 1927 and originally housed a tea room and the headquarters of Great Western Railway operations west of Taunton; D&C had been there since 1964.

Renowned for its railway and canal books, the company was established on April Fool's Day 1960 by journalist, broadcaster and railway enthusiast David St John Thomas and his business partner Charles Hadfield, a colleague experienced in both commercial and government publishing and a 'canal man.' Significantly, both were members of the Railway and Canal Historical Society.

Operating from a small bedroom at first and for ten months of 1964 from "a hut in the garden," the fledgling company found its turnover jump from £16,000 to £56,000 in just one year as – Mr Thomas wrote in an exceptionally frank 1977 article in *The Bookseller* – "we discovered the market for solid books of local interest."

The "rocky patch" of 1975 was presaged when the 1973 war in the Middle East ignited a chain of economic events at home that rocked the stock market; this was followed by raging inflation, killing the chances of D&C going public, and its finances were further constrained by the needs of its Readers Union book club.

But, in a complex scenario of good fortune, outside help and determination, matters turned around and four years later the company was back in profit with a group turnover of some £4 million. In 1981 D&C celebrated its 21st birthday by publishing a coffee table-style paperback *Good Books Come From Devon*, a title summing up the company's ethos perfectly.

One delightful anecdote from this entertaining book read: "We quickly lost one member of Readers Union after taking over the book club in 1971. A butler wrote an angry letter saying that her ladyship was annoyed the postman could see she belonged to a club and thought we would have been intelligent enough to mail books to titled people in plain wrapping."

D&C designers at work in the Brunel House offices

A market leader in illustrated non-fiction, the David & Charles brand became synonymous with books on Britain's canals and railways, yet the company's ownership has changed several times in recent years. It was bought out by American company F+W Media in 2019, is now based in Exeter and promotes online learning courses, including a botanical course through The Royal Botanic Gardens, Kew and an embroidery course through the Royal School of Needlework "for aspiring embroiderers worldwide."

The site of its former home in Brunel Road is now a branch of supermarket Aldi and an extensive Railway Studies Collection is housed on the first floor of the Passmore Edwards library building in Market Street, Newton Abbot. Accessible from 9am-4pm, Monday-Saturday this archive of books, photographs and slides, is supported by a Friends group and all aspects of the country's railways are covered "with material of interest to railway and social historians, writers, modellers, researchers and those with a more general interest." There is comprehensive material "on West Country Railways from the Great Western and London South Western/Southern periods up to the present day" and a substantial amount of information on the remainder of the UK's railway network. The Friends meet regularly and members help finance new additions to the collection that includes material donated by David St John Thomas who died in 2014.

D&C leased the site of these bombed houses to build its Brunel House offices. The former Railway Cottages were demolished after a German raid on the station in 1940 that erupted just as a train bound for Plymouth was passing

Merry-go-Roundabout

The Penn Inn roundabout opened on 20 May, 1975. Immediately Newton Abbot Trades Council complained that the pedestrian subways were incomplete and it was extremely dangerous for pedestrians to cross such a busy junction to access the Penn Inn swimming pool.

The subways were finally opened in July and walkers were advised to use them instead of dodging the traffic, to which they had presumably become accustomed. Town councillors were told the same month that building the roundabout had made the junction of Queensway and Shaldon Road 'a death trap.'

Long before the great roundabout, work was instigated in August 1963 to demolish the Acton Works factory at Penn Inn to make way for a major improvement to Torquay Road. Six large petrol tanks, reminders of the pre-war days when the factory was used as a filling station, were removed to be used by the county council to store diesel.

In early 1991 traffic monitoring cameras were installed at Penn Inn and in their first four months caught more than 500 drivers going through red lights.

Building works carried on after the Penn Inn roundabout opened in May, 1975

Of Pantomime Horses and Liverpool Merchants: TV comedy comes to Newton Abbot

The odds were on that no tipsters would be backing any of the mounts attempting the jumps at Newton Abbot Racecourse on 21 April, 1976 – as they were all pantomime horses.

For Tim Brooke-Taylor, Graeme Garden and Bill Oddie – *The Goodies* – had come to town to film sequences for the fourth episode of their sixth hit BBC TV sit-com. That episode, *Black and White Beauty*, was due for an autumn screening and was eventually broadcast on 12 October, that year.

I had been a big fan of the radio series *I'm Sorry, I'll Read That Again* that starred all three of them, along with John Cleese, David Hatch and Jo Kendall and while Graham sadly told me there would be no further episodes of that iconic show it was still a great pleasure to meet the three of them. Bill, I saw, spent most of the time darting around monitoring the scenes while Graham and Tim waited patiently to be given their cues for "action!"

The trio were at the racecourse for two days and planned to get some sequences in the can at the Buckfastleigh racecourse as well. One scene already captured was a skit of blockbuster big shark movie *Jaws* filmed at Rickmansworth Aquadrome, Hertfordshire, with a mock 20ft cod as the star prop. The entourage comprised a film crew, extras, special effects specialists Peter Day and Tony Harding and their team, and a pantechnicon of props. Shaping the scenes was director Jim Franklin.

Graeme Garden, resting between takes in the bottom half of a pantomime horse costume, explained the process: "We are doing seven shows, which is about five weeks' filming," he said. "Then we do the shows once a week in the studio," those scenes recorded in front of an invited audience.

The day before, some of the cast of the BBC's popular nautical serial *The Onedin Line* had also been in town. Taking a break from filming at Dartmouth for a new series due to start its run the following week, the crew came to a house called Montmillan, in Seymour Road, aiming to show the residence of a Liverpool merchant. But it was not until they arrived that they realised that was just what they had found! The house was built in 1890 and in 1908 it was bought by Liverpool architect R.H. Roberts, who retired there, changing its name from Trecoven. The fascinated cast were told the tale by the late architect's grandson, Neville Roberts.

The By-Pass From Hell

Close to one hundred people turned out on 17 May, 1976 to see county council chairman Cllr Charles Ansell cut the tape to formally open what had turned out to be Devon's most costly by-pass of the period. A year behind schedule and £2.5 million over budget – rising from £5.5 million to £8 million in three years – the Newton Abbot project was hit by more than its fair share of snags.

As if to echo an unspoken thought from the public that they had lived with the whole thing for just a little too long, the chairman of contractors Peter Lind, T.M. Jaeger, admitted at the ceremony that the task of building the three-and-a-quarter mile long highway had been "a very difficult job. There have, indeed, been occasions when one wondered whether or not it would even be finished."

The need for a by-pass had been agreed some time before the actual route was accepted in 1967. Because of its departure from the county development plan, the project needed Ministry approval – and got it in 1972. The main contractor, Peter Lind, was appointed and work started in 1973. By August, the residents of Chichester Estate were complaining about late-night working. A 7am-7pm working day had been agreed, but one resident, a postman, claimed: "I left for work one morning this week at 4.30am and they were working then!"

The first major hold-up was in May 1974 when shattered rock was discovered in the Teign viaduct foundations and the contractors were forced to bed down more piling to support the piers. This was the central cause of the one-year delay.

In August a plan to introduce new rock-blasting methods to speed up the process was dropped because of county council concerns about the resultant noise.

In January 1975 a faulty section of the Ware Barton bridge had to be replaced due to serious cracking and an article in *Construction News* suggested: "Reinforcement drawings are believed to have been read the wrong way round."

In April one of the sub-contractors permanently pulled their earth-moving vehicles out of the scheme over a pay row. Another sub-contractor decided to forego a £42,000 road surfacing contract in November following a dispute and in December the vice-chairman of Teignbridge Council, Cllr Leonard Lamb, called for an inquiry into the work because of the mounting delays.

During construction more than 1.2 million cubic meters of material was removed, much of it used for filling in embankments. The 1,100 yard long Humber Lane cutting was 85ft deep from its highest point. The viaduct alone cost £1.3 million and was built with eleven spans over the quarter-mile channel between banks.

The twin carriageways were each 24ft wide with each lane spanning 12ft and separated by a 15ft central reservation.

The Bridge That Went Down in a Day

Newton Abbot's bow-shaped railway bridge in Torquay Road was blown up on Sunday 6 March, 1977 to make way for a modern substitution. West-bound trains terminated at Newton Abbot and passengers bound for Totnes, Plymouth and Paignton were taken to their destinations by bus. Two 150ft cranes towered two 100ft girders into place as the basis of a new span bridge.

The landmark girder bridge was more than a century old, from a time when its builders really knew a thing or two about working with iron. But excessive traffic had put a strain on the elderly structure, requiring its replacement with a modern steel alternative and at 6am 56lbs of explosives placed overnight in the foundations brought down some 300 tons of stonework to be taken away by awaiting rail wagons. The area was cleared within 24hrs and the new bridge assembled two weeks' later on Sunday 20 March.

One of British Rail's inter-city 125 high-speed trains made its passenger-carrying debut on Easter Sunday, 10 April, bringing day trippers from London to Plymouth. A prototype 125 had travelled to Plymouth before, but only on a test run.

Vroom! That Was the Queen, That Was

They dubbed her the 'high-speed Queen' – but Her Majesty's swift Silver Jubilee trip through Kingskerswell, Newton Abbot and Kingsteignton on 5 August, 1977 was by no means diminished for the huge crowds who turned out to wish her well.

The area had celebrated the 25th anniversary of her reign in fine style in June and Newton Abbot Town Council had even minted a special crown for the occasion. So, stuffed with anticipation, people lined the streets, hung from window ledges and leaned over rooftop parapets to see – no matter how briefly – the Queen and Duke of Edinburgh zoom past in their gleaming black limousine.

The Royal motorcade was late leaving Torbay, where the Royal Yacht Britannia had been moored for this leg of HM's Jubilee tour of Devon. There had been fears that she would merely swish up the A380 by-pass, missing both Newton Abbot and Kingsteignton completely – but these were unfounded, although she passed through Kingskerswell in less than two minutes.

At the Lemon Road junction in Newton, crowds surged into the road almost mobbing the Royal car, then already about ten minutes behind schedule on its planned route to Exeter.

Waiting was an official tiered platform in Courtenay Street containing civic dignitaries. But the Queen whisked by with barely a glance in their direction: she was more interested in the children on the other side of the road dressed in patriotic clothes and waving Union Jacks. The cars slowed near the racecourse where youth groups, the elderly and disabled were stationed, and then moved off to The Fountain and Eagle Farm by-pass junction. In the afternoon trip to Haldon race track there were two firsts: the Queen and Prince Philip drove up the course in an open landau drawn by four greys – the first time outside Ascot; it was also the first visit to the course by a reigning monarch.

The Queen's limo takes the Queen Street junction at Lloyds Bank at a fair lick. Note the former Dingles branch and gents' outfitters Laws and Wareham in the background. Below, the jubilant crowds on that corner that caught her eye.

It Wasn't You...

Three local lotteries were set up in Newton Abbot between September 1977 and October 1988. One lasted just three months, another eight months and the third eleven months. In the first of the trio, Teignbridge Council started its own lottery, raising £3,300 in the opening month and selling 28,000 tickets. Spurred on by this success, football team Newton Abbot Dynamos instigated its own lottery in November which folded in October 1988.

Newton Abbot Town Council also had a go, kicking off their attempt in April 1978. It employed a manager with 72 sellers and set up its own booth at Millets Corner (*pictured*); some 25,000 tickets were printed, also farmed out to local stores and newsagents. In the first lottery, 10,626 tickets were sold with a loss of £100 and the £750 first prize was not claimed. The scheme collapsed in June after just three draws with the loss of £1,129.04. In April 1978 Teignbridge Council discussed turning to Instants as its own lottery was losing impetus, but the whole thing was suspended three months later.

The Leper Home

In November 1977 it was learned that Gilberd's Almshouses in Exeter Road were to be demolished and the two remaining families housed there were found council accommodation at Broadlands.

Founded during the reign of Henry VIII in 1538 by Exeter burgess John Gilberd, the almshouses were first used to house a leper colony, but after renovation in 1657 they were made available to the poor and aged from the parish of Highweek. The building was in the care of the Highweek Feoffees and was entirely rebuilt in 1852. Lady Baker, of nearby Sandford Orleigh, would send a sheep's head there three times a week and celebrated both Christmas Day and her birthday by giving residents presents of butter, tea and cake.

In May 1979 eight flats costing £70,000 to build were opened on the 1852 site (the original site being nearer Foxwell Lane). The change had been planned by the Feoffees for several years, but they could not proceed until permission was granted by the Charity Commission and the Housing Corporation.

The town's oldest almshouses, in East Street, were founded by Elizabethan philanthropist Robert Hayman and rebuilt by the Feoffees in 1840.

Coffee Break

CARWARDINES

Does fresh ground coffee post free, taste like a good idea?

CARWARDINES COFFEE PRICES DOWN

Now you can enjoy fresh Carwardines coffee at home. Because, we'll post it to you free of charge. So your coffee will cost you exactly the same as it would if our shops. And you'll have saved time, and travelling expenses. It will taste just as good, because we'll send it in heat-sealed packets, to keep in the flavour. Pop it in the refrigerator straight away and it will stay fresh longer.

Choose from these delicious blends

Connoisseur: One of our most popular blends, suitable for any occasion

Westminster: A good robust breakfast coffee

Brazilian: South American style

Minimum order of 2lbs of fresh coffee £5.64 postage paid (£2.82 per lb)

Tick whether you require your coffee:
- Loose beans ☐
- Fine ground filter ☐
- Coarse ground for percolator ☐

Tick blend and state quantities required

Blend	Quantities
Connoisseur ☐	☐ lbs.
Westminster ☐	☐ lbs.
Brazilian ☐	☐ lbs.

Name.

Address

Dept MDA 9

Send cheque/PO To Stephen Carwardine & Co Ltd, 93 Union St, Torquay TQ1 3DW. Valid for all orders received by Aug 12, '77

The kind of newspaper advertisements we looked at in 1977

On Our Bikes

In August 1978, Teignbridge Magistrates began hearing charges against motorcycle protesters who were refusing to comply with a new law making the wearing of helmets compulsory.

The bikers said they were not against wearing helmets *per se* – just against it being made mandatory; particularly as, at the time, there was no comparable legislation for car drivers on the buckling of seat belts – and some refused to pay court fines.

A huge protest rally organised by the Motorcycle Action Group was staged in Newton Abbot on 21 October when over 3,000 bikers from all over the country packed the narrow streets.

They gathered at the Penn Inn swimming pool area in the early afternoon before forming a three-mile procession through the town centre, cheered by crowds and shepherded by police motorcycle outriders (themselves wearing helmets).

After a tour of Torbay the protesters returned to Newton Abbot bringing toys for a children's home as a gesture of good will.

In one hearing seven motor-cyclists appeared before Teignbridge Magistrates on a total of 26 charges of not wearing a helmet and their spokesman, 69-year-old Fred Hill, of the MAG, told the hearing that the law was 'patently unjust and administratively unfair.'

Helmets deprived riders of their sense of hearing and sight to a great degree and it would be unworthy to make criminals of them them, he said.

But chairman of the bench Cllr Leonard Lamb responded that it was the duty of the court to uphold the law and urged the bikers to pay up and to make their representations to Parliament.

Bailing In

A bail hostel, the first of its kind in the South West, opened its doors at 13 Devon Square, Newton Abbot, on 23 January, 1978 despite a hostile public reaction, an attitude that continued for most of its 16-year history.

Councillors, planning officers, some doctors and police officers, nearby residents and the general rank and file were adamant that they did not want the hostel to be established, for fear of adverse effects. Petitions were gathered and lodged, but to no avail.

The idea to create such a place – to provide short-term accommodation for youngsters over seventeen, released on bail by the courts – was first mooted in December 1974. But the project, then targeted at 2 South Road, was vetoed by a government inspector at a public inquiry in February 1975.

Opposition to a second application in early 1976 for the Grade II Devon Square property was dashed in December when the go-ahead was announced following a second public inquiry in October. Devon Probation Service bought the building in 1977 and converted it from a private residence.

The 12-bailee hostel, later renovated to accommodate 16 residents, was officially opened on January 28, 1978 by the Bishop of Crediton, the Rt Revd Philip Pasterfield, and named the Dudley Centre after the late Kenneth Dudley, who had been a senior probation officer in South Devon. It finally stopped admitting new residents in March 1994 and closed shortly afterwards. It was put on the market in December 1994.

✂ Snippets #3 – the Musical Notes

Supercalifragalistic-anditsattheAlex

The world stage premiere of *Mary Poppins* was held at the Alexandra Theatre by Newton Abbot and District Musical Comedy Society in November 1978. Adapted from the film script by local journalist Jonathan Dumble and produced by his mother Queenie Dumble, the spirited show attracted more advance bookings than any other production in the society's 64-year history.

Longa Conga? Wronga!

A world record conga attempt was staged in the town, on 19 August, 1978, but only 200 people turned up for the challenge, less than four per cent of the 5,562 required. It made £52 but, after expenses had been met, the grand sum of £1 was left to share between the Save The Children Fund and the 4th Newton Abbot Cubs.

All Together Now

A floral dance made its way through the town centre on 6 May, 1978 led by the Coombeshead School Band and including pupils from the Cynthia Vittles and Gaynor Walter schools of dance. Part of the reason for the colourful parade was the first draw in the town lottery after 11,000 tickets had been sold.

Norse Brass

More than one hundred Norwegian youngsters marched through the town on 19 June, 1978. Members of the Konnerud and Eidanger youth bands were parping off the Devon leg of their trip to England with a Newton Abbot procession during carnival week.

Are You Lonesome tonight?

Some 150 fans from Newton Abbot crammed into St Paul's Church Hall on 16 August, 1978 to commemorate the first anniversary of the death of the King of Rock and Roll. They wore badges marked *Elvis Presley 1935-1977 RIP*, listened to his greatest records and observed a one-minute's silence. A spontaneous collection raised £9 for church funds.

Tanks for the Memories

Tanks of the 3rd Royal Tank Regiment rumbled through Newton Abbot in April 1979 as part of a ceremonial visit to the area.

Always game for a challenge, Town Mayor Cllr Mrs Frances Humpherson took a turn in the commander's hatch.

Crossing Now – Seven Elephants

There's nothing more likely to stall a driving lesson than coming across a herd of Indian elephants. But that's what happened to driver Les Flower and his instructor Freda Newlyn in May 1979. The patient pachyderm party was beginning a trunk-to-trunk parade through the town with three keepers to promote Fossett's Circus at the Racecourse.

SHOULD this country re-introduce capital punishment? Is the death penalty the ultimate deterrent to the wave of violent crimes?

These were some of the questions the 'Advertiser' asked when it conducted a snap poll in Newton Abbot on Friday.

Fifteen out of 19 people to whom we spoke favoured the return of the death penalty. The others were against its re-introduction.

(1977)

New Lamps For Old

Two rare Victorian lamps which had been used as gas lights before electricity came to the town in 1921 were declared unsafe by Devon County Council in June 1979 and were removed because they couldn't be repaired.

They were taken from East Street to a museum in Hertfordshire.

The Victorian lamp is the one on the right – as if you needed telling that…

Decoy Park: Hovercrafty...
Plus: A Lake? No, Thank you

Secret trials of a hovercraft with revolutionary steering equipment allowing greater manoeuvrability took place on Decoy Lake in October 1979.

It belonged to Sector Hovercrafts and was being filmed by BBC TV for its *Brainwave* programme. The machine was originally being tested in the Teign Estuary but was moved to Decoy after it caught a riverside post and the skirting was ripped.

But there could have been NO eleven-acre lake at Decoy for it to glide across if local residents had gotten their way back in January 1970.

Experts spent most of a two-hour meeting with nearby home owners trying to talk them out of their demands that the former quarry of clay company Watts Blake Bearne be filled in as they were fearful that their homes would slide into the water.

The council had planned to make the area a nature reserve until an application for a caravan site west of the quarry fell through because the land was potentially unstable. Council officers promised concerned residents that the £6,000-plus project to stabilise the banks and surrounding land would make the lake safe for two years. But they were still told: "We want the lake filled in completely."

But attitudes had changed by March 1975. Devon's amenities and countryside committee gave the go-ahead to turn the 29-acre site into a recreational area at a cost of around £30,000. The lake went on to be celebrated as well as used by Newton Abbot Sailing Club.

In October 1977 police frogmen searched the waters for a missing schoolgirl who was later found safe and well. Decoy Park inherited the old Penn Inn park gates in November and six of the eight pairs of black swans resident at Dawlish were brought to the lake to encourage them to breed.

Badge of Flowers

Newton Abbot St John Ambulance Cadets celebrated their Silver Jubilee in August 1979 with a special floral display in Courtenay Park, opposite the railway station. They created their badge in a colourful cluster of blooms using some 22,000 bedding plants.

Royal Accolade for Newton Writer

Prolific and popular local author Judy Chard published one of her most celebrated books, *Along the River Lemon*, in November 1978.

In it she wrote that the watercourse "has been bearing its soft, peaty water to the Teign since the Bronze Age, for near the springs in Bagtor Mire where one tributary, the Sig, rises, there are hut circles where once an agricultural site stood…"

The book was read and applauded by a huge audience – including HM Queen Elizabeth II.

In January 1979 the author received a letter from Buckingham Palace that read: "I am commanded by The Queen to thank you for your charming present *Along the Lemon* which Her Majesty has read with great interest.

"The chapter about Ogwell Mill is particularly interesting in view of the fact that it is owned by Lieutenant-Commander and Mrs Holdsworth. How lucky you are to live in that part of the World!"

Snippets #4

Lincoln Lung

In 1976 Teignbridge Council began mulling over turning Victoria Place, Newton Abbot, into a 'Green Lung.' The idea of chief district planning officer Noel Dann, the project was aimed at providing 'a breath of fresh air' with a place to relax. Though overshadowed somewhat by the imposing Crown building built on the site of the town's bus station across the river, the area flourished and Victoria Gardens, as it is now known, was given a major upgrade by Newton Abbot Town Council in 2013 incorporating paving, lighting, seats, trees, grassed areas and glass sections in the river wall giving views of the watercourse and protected by security cameras (*pictured below*).

A Rum Do

Three times Grand National winner Red Rum made an appearance for the opening of a new bar at Newton Abbot Racecourse on 2 July, 1978 during the Country Sports Show. The chance to see this 13-year-old vintage horse drew over 8,000 people to the event, twice as many as attended the show in 1977.

Woodland For All

Devon County Council bought 165 acres of Forestry Commission Land in March 1979 – comprising Newpark and Blacksticks plantations and Stover Lake. Part of the former Stover Estate, the land needed a further £47,000 spent on it to provide a road access, car park and toilets.

Quite a Beating

The beating of the bounds of Newton Abbot was revived in April 1979, and walkers embraced the challenge for the first time since 1954.

About one hundred eager souls set out from Bradley Manor on the first of the two-day weekend event, culminating in an evening of folk dancing in the Newfoundland Way car park.

The youngest bounds beater was twenty-month-old Melissa Dawn Tunnicliffe and the youngest walker was four-year-old Daniel McCandlish who completed the section between the manor and Bracewell Field. In line with tradition, an eight-year-old, Marina Gaskell, was bounced on the boundary stone at Mallands Lane, and Town Mayor Cllr Nancy Morrison was given an unscheduled 'trial bumping' before the start of the event.

Giving Up the Ghost

I reported the meetings of Newton Abbot Town Council regularly in the 1970s – and on into the eighties and nineties. I always found its members a mostly delightful bunch of dedicated and diligent representatives of townsfolk, their wards and their needs, and were even prepared to laugh at themselves if matters warranted – as witnessed by the cartoon and story on the next page.

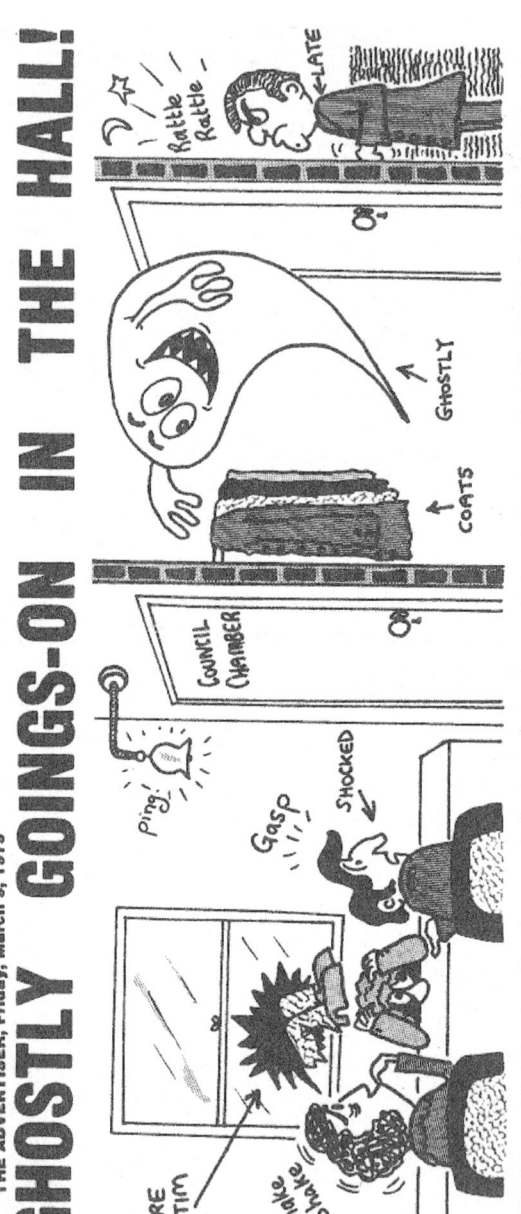

Quoted in my book The Other Side of the Ribbon (A scrapbook of eccentric adventures in local newspaper offices)

Keep Watching the Skies

South Devon had its own small wave of UFO sightings near the end of 1979, leading on to quite a spate in the early eighties, many of them reported in the *Mid-Devon Advertiser*.

Reporter of the day Mike Beevers wrote a number of the stories and I compiled a handful of UFO sighting sheets including details of caller, date and time of the incident and the prevailing weather conditions. Included in the eventual bundle of those 1979 sightings were these.

In November 1979, an area youth officer and his daughter spotted a red light in the skies over Teignmouth which flashed up and down, turned blue and white and disappeared – only to reappear over Dartmoor. Considered too large to be an aeroplane, and silent, these "lights flashed up and down in a vertical line" moving "in an arc from the north to the west and then vanished in the south."

A week later came more reports of strange lights from five other readers, one of whom saw "a large ball" in the Dartmoor skies near Bovey Tracey. It was "bigger than a jumbo jet and hovered up and down and turned blue and white before moving south." In early December a cluster of hovering lights "that resembled an ambulance light or discotheque lights that flashed about once every second" were seen by three Hennock residents.

In June 1980 there were several more sightings: a "long silver line" of lights followed by about thirteen smaller lights were observed from Heathfield and a UFO "shaped like a cross" was seen over Dartmoor by two policemen, one retired, and a Teignmouth harbour pilot. The Ministry of Defence reported "no night-flying activities over Dartmoor on the night in question." In August Stephen Beard and girlfriend spotted three cigar-shaped objects over Poundsgate. His comedian father, Widecombe Wag Tony Beard said it was "no gag from the Wag. It frightened the living daylights out of them."

Identified terrestrial 'saucer:' Avro Canada's distinctively-shaped 1950s VZ-9-AV Avrocar, an attempt to create a supersonic, vertical take-off and landing fighter-bomber

Whether or not these seventies incidents were influenced in any way by members of the 'upper house' is hard to say, but the Lords had a lengthy evening debate on Unidentified Flying Objects on 18 January, 1979 led by Nicholas Power Richard Le Poer Trench, 9th Earl of Clancarty and nephew of the late 8th Earl, prodigious UFO writer Brinsley Le Poer Trench.

After detailing a number of 'astounding reports,' the hereditary peer advised his fellows that "this worldwide UFO invasion of every country's air space is of growing importance and therefore I suggest that Parliament keeps a continuous watch on the situation."

Most members took the matter fairly seriously, even those who admitted they had never seen a UFO, as they were especially concerned about retaining the security of British airspace, whatever these odd objects turned out to be – alien, Russian or swamp gas.

Yet at one point in the debate Lord Davies of Leek reported he had been told "that an ambassador of 8ft 6ins with green feet and webbed feet as well had asked whether he could park his flying saucer in our car park." This was "according to some of the telephones that have been ringing here today, because some people have treated the whole matter as a joke."

Certainly most of those reporting their local experiences of unusual activities in the skies to their local paper back in the seventies and eighties seemed both sincere and rather taken aback by their experiences.

And the appearances of mysterious lights – and even apparently solid objects – in the skies around the world have continued, 44 years later in 2023.

They remain just as mysterious and unexplained.

Beings from space 'did not kill ponies'

THE Dartmoor Livestock Protection Society has ruled out extra-terrestrial intervention in the mysterious deaths of 15 Dartmoor ponies found near Postbridge.

Ina statement the society says it has reason to believe that the ponies "did not die as a result of redworm infestation, nor as the result of flooding, extra-terrestrial activity or poisoning by bog asphodel.

"Neither does it accept the likelihood of the dumping of these carcasses so widely dispersed through a quarter mile terrain affording difficult access."

The mystery was probed by a Devon UFO team two weeks ago but the investigation failed to shel any light on the deaths.

The protection society's secretary, Mrs J. Wilson, said: "We pretty well know what happened, but we have to be very careful what we say. We think they came to a violent end, but we don't think it came from outer space.

"Our problem is going to be and has been all along, that it is doubtful that we will have sufficient hard and fast information to name names without the risk of libel.

"The ponies weer cetrtainly either terrorised or stampeded. There is quite a bit of evidence accrued now which we haven't talked about at this stage."

The whole mystery is expected to be explained as fully as possible during the next few weeks. The society, with the Animal Defence Authority, will be holding a press conference in the near future at either Postbridge or Tavistock.

Cutting from 1977 (Herald Express)

The Last Great Flood

1 The Build-Up: Remembering 1938

The long, hot summer of 1975 reached drought proportions by the summer of 1976 and water from Decoy Lake was used to serve parched local nurseries. Standpipes were due to be implemented from 15 September 1976 and South West Water banned baptismal baths because of the serious conditions. This ironically followed the 1970 floods and a 1972 inundation of Newton Abbot Racecourse.

When the high tides and melting snow of February 1978 threatened the town with flooding, locals looked back with concern at the 1938 floods – so striking that few had forgotten them, even if they had not been old enough to have to personally experienced the episode. After all, there had also been significant flooding in the town on 19 December, 1853 and 14 November, 1894 – let alone the 1970 torrent that began the decade – and it was beginning to look like a serious, recurring event.

As the October 26, 1979 *Advertiser* reported, looking cautiously back in time... 'Between 5am and 10am on Thursday August 4, 1938 rainfall was registered at Seale-Hayne College, Newton Abbot as 4.35 inches. From 10am to 3pm a further 0.52 of an inch fell, making a total of 4.87 inches in ten hours. What was referred to at the time as "a thunderstorm of unparalleled intensity in living memory" actually broke at 3am, beginning a "night of terror" and causing thousands of pounds' worth of stock damage, flooding to a depth of several feet and the death of a number of animals.

'Even those with experience of tropical rainstorms were said never to have encountered such a terrifying experience, for lightning and thunder continued almost without a break. The storm was so fierce that when it became necessary to summon the town's fire brigade, at about 7am, two distress maroons were discharged in case the first had not been heard over the noise..."

The report went on: 'In the ten-hour nightmare, animals died, homes were seriously damaged, farmland flooded, telephones cut off, thunderbolts struck homes, rail services were cut, houses were hit by lightning and the rising waters swept through thousands of pounds' worth of personal and business property.'

In 1979, the matter that triggered the re-telling of the 1938 incident was a controversial plan to build up to 1,000 homes at Ogwell Cross. The man who took the 1938 photographs, renowned photographer A. Vincent Bibbings, warned of further tragedy if developers went ahead with their plans, adding: "It could happen again – and it would be much more likely to happen if they had that development on that side of town."

Flood waters hit Bank Street in 1938
(also next page)

That 1978 summer was a strikingly hot one, lingering on well into the autumn and a hosepipe ban was imposed on Teignbridge from 4 November. Yet weekend blizzards hit the area in January 1979 – a precursor of what was to come as the year, and the decade, drew to a close. In timely fashion, Mr Bibbings' fears expressed to the *Advertiser* in October that the 1938 floods could be repeated came true. And on Thursday, 27 December...

2 The Disaster

It was dubbed the worst flood disaster in the history of the town and, whilst no-one was killed or injured, the damage was extensive and ran into millions of pounds.

Dartmoor was saturated by heavy rains and the run-off had nowhere else to go than down the valley into Newton Abbot. In two days, 26 and 27 December, over seven inches of rain fell and by 7pm on the 27th the River Lemon was a torrent. The culvert that runs for more than 1,000ft under the town centre could not cope, despite its capacity to handle 35 cubic meters of water each second – around 665 million gallons a day.

A commanding cascade burst the banks of the Lemon, the force of the water and the debris it carried tearing a 40ft hole in the boundary wall and forcing 3ft of water into Linden Terrace homes. Residents of The Avenue heard the flood water rushing under their houses even before it reached their front doors and carried on inside their properties.

The town centre looked like a lake with businesses in Highweek Street, Bank Street and Courtenay Street under several feet of water and the new market square awash.

The town centre turns into a river, 1979

Despite having its floor re-laid in 1972 two inches above the 1938 flood level, shoe shop Ridgeway in Bank Street was still flooded, to a depth of 2ft 9in. Austins escaped unscathed as twenty staff had made the building virtually watertight earlier in the evening with carpets, sacks and paper bags. Their work was so successful that the store was able to open for business the morning after, while other shop staffs were trying to mop up the debris.

Substantial damage was caused to the Recreational Trust in Marsh Road, with its squash courts ruined and the new bar under water; damage to cars amounting to six figures was recorded by the Seymour Horwell garage and Newton Abbot Motors in Wolborough Street; at the racecourse the old trainers' stand collapsed and the new grandstand and offices were flooded.

Almost the entire town was blacked out, with the main power cut lasting over six hours. SWEB had pulled the switch because of the danger of inundation to the sub-stations, but most supplies were restored by late Friday night.

Police set up road blocks and buses were switched to Torquay as Newton Abbot bus station was under 3ft of water. Police, fire and ambulance services, along with council workers, Teignmouth coastguards and the Royal Marines, worked through the night to tackle the crisis.

What Newton Abbot's long-departed bus station looked like, with the River Lemon and Victoria Place (right), taken from the roof of the multi-storey car park in Sherborne Road

An emergency relief centre was set up by the town council in the afternoon, before the inundation; initially at the scout hall in Wolborough Street it was transferred across the road to St Leonard's

Church due to the impending threat of worse to come.

Those rescued from their saturated homes were taken to a police-designated relief centre at Coombeshead School. It catered for about fifty, with meals supplied by the WRVS and Red Cross and beds by Newton Abbot Round Table, whose members also provided a food van for the Osborne Park area. Relief work was hampered by the lack of telephones – hit first by the waters and then gale force winds.

The former gasometers at the junction of Lemon Road and The Avenue reflected in a playing field lake of flood water

3 Aftermath

On the morning after the town was caked with an inches-thick layer of mud. The bridge in The Avenue was checked for structural damage on Friday afternoon by county council divers and re-opened with an all-clear 24 hours later.

After an inspection of the aftermath, Teignbridge Council announced the setting-up of a flood disaster appeal fund, with the authority contributing £10,000.

Staff of the Queen Street Co-op carry out their part in the inevitable and heartbreaking shops clear-up

During the emergency forty workmen with fifteen lorries from the county and district councils worked flat out, with extra men and materials drafted in from the M5 motorway, East Devon, Tiverton, Crediton and Plymouth. And, as if the flooding was not enough, the next three evenings were spent salting the roads as the weather turned icy cold.

Over 700 buildings were flooded in the incident and loss and damage amounted to £800,000 for residential properties and £2.8 million for commercial premises. Ironically, South West Water's local land drainage committee had given the thumbs-up just one month earlier for its officials to produce a flood relief scheme for the town.

Embankments and walls were subsequently built along the River Lemon at Albany Street, Victoria Place and the former power station land off The Avenue.

4 Never again...

More importantly, the Holbeam Dam was built, in a high-speed project between July 1981 and March 1982. Costing more than £400,000 and with a storage capacity of 90 million gallons, it was designed to contain water flow through use of a radial gate to prevent such a devastating and uncontrollable cascade in future years.

Holbeam Dam, 1982: the four metre galvanised steel inlet screen blocked rubble, trees and vegetation from being carried downstream

The dam entered civil engineering history by becoming the first in Britain to be built in unbounded rolled concrete – a mix of cement, aggregate and water which led to speedier laying. Both Devon Contractors and South West Water agreed that a conventional concrete dam would have been an intrusion in the countryside.

It crossed the Lemon valley at Holbeam close to the home of local author Judy Chard. Landscaped soon after its completion it contained a 40,000 cubic metre concrete core covered with around 9,000 cubic metres of earth.

In many subsequent years the dam has been praised for saving the town from being swamped again. In 1992 alone it held back some 18 million gallons. And, to date, Newton Abbot has not suffered further serious flooding.

There have been only two occasions when the dam experienced 'overtopping.' The most recent was in 1982 during 'Storm Dennis' – on Sunday, 16 February, by approximately 150mm at 6.20am, its highest recorded level. The spillway is some 24ft from the ground and the £30,000 radial gate helps shut off flows, containing the water behind the dam.

Storm Dennis caused road flooding and landslips throughout the county. Locally, water encroached on to the A383 and A381, roads leading to Teigngrace were deluged, and the level of the River Lemon rose, cutting off some local footpaths.

But the dam still did its job, remained stable and controlled downstream flows, reducing any major risk to the town, and whist there were numerous blocked drains no homes were urgently evacuated.

Officials had finally heeded the stark warning that came with that 1979 deluge – and we end this little book where we started, with a cautionary reprimand in the voice of the River Lemon itself.

In a final chapter of author Judy Chard's Royally-approved paperback, *Along the Lemon*, her neighbour Owen Caunter (whose upstream home was inundated in the 1938 flood) wrote a telling open letter to the town planners, in the voice of the Lemon: *I Am a River – It Wasn't My Fault*.

He concluded his account of the tumbling rampage from Haytor Quarries, racing down the valley and uncontrollably crashing through the centre of the town, like this:

"What I think you should have done was to build a bigger culvert for me before you built this new market. You had a golden opportunity then, but you'll have to do something before I come down in flood again. Maybe this year... maybe next... maybe not for fifty years... but I'm sure I'll be back. Sorry folks... don't blame me."

The End

Because of the daily clash between incoming tide and downhill outflow, plus other factors such as soil erosion, the Lemon needs to be regularly cleared of silt. Such a clean-up is pictured (above) at The Avenue's road bridge in 1972, between the two great floods.

Postscript...

POST DATE

NEWTON Abbot's new post office will open on September 3, provided there are no snags.

One innovation will be a single - queueing system, where customers line up behind a barrier and only move forward to the counter when a widow becomes free.

Newton Abbot Postmaster Mr George Patey said this week: 'The system has been introduced in many other offices with great success. It gives the customer greater privacy and it does ensure that everyone is served in turn.'

The new post office will have one long counter and will be bigger than its older Bearnes Lane brother — due to be demolished later in the year.

Many hated the introduction of client-controlling "sheep pens" in its new post office, opened in October 1979.

But they generally welcomed the 2,500 sq ft building in Market Square, launched in the company's 'customer care year.'

Postmaster George Patey said. "People new to the town will be able to find us much more easily than before when the Bearnes Lane premises was tucked away off the beaten track."

Sadly, the unit has been boarded up and empty since the facility relocated to the Costcutter convenience store in lower Queen Street some two decades ago.

Teignbridge Council bought the empty building in 2016 for a reported £13 million.

The single - queue system in operation on the opening day of Newton Abbot's new post office.

The Final Pieces: 2023
'Chips' Barber,
Paul Theroux,
Cllr Di Nicholls;
The Mid-Devon Advertiser,
Books by Brian Thomas

'Chips' Barber

Chips and Sally Barber

This book originated as *Newton Abbot in the News*, the central volume of a proposed trio of books covering developments in the town and its surrounds in the sixties, seventies and eighties. The only volume completed and now long out of print, *Newton Abbot in the News* was produced by Obelisk Publications, of Pinhoe, Exeter in 1996 while I was still chief reporter of the Newton-based weekly newspaper the *Mid-Devon Advertiser*.

I was commissioned by Obelisk founder, the late Chips Barber, to add my input to his extraordinary series of 'local' books, each customarily comprising 32 pages in an A5 format with lots of pictures and covering wide-ranging subjects, mostly written by Chips and designed and typeset by his wife Sally.

A multitude of fascinating and popular titles included Derek Beavis's *The Templar Way*, *TV Programmes, Films and Adverts… Made in Devon*, co-authored by Chips and David Fitzgerald, and Chips's own *Great Little Dartmoor Book*, *Diary of a Dartmoor Walker*, *The Haldon Hills Revisited* as well as, with Sally, *Haunted Pubs in Devon* and *Ten Family Walks on Dartmoor* – and many, many more. His first outing was *Around and About the Haldon Hills*.

A former teacher, Chips was a keen walker and latterly president of the Devon Ramblers' Association. He was much in demand as a public speaker and was a regular contributor to BBC Radio Devon.

The company was set up in 1982 by Chips and Sally and their range of subjects and host of information contained in each book was extraordinary, their output running to some 240 titles. Sadly Chips died in 2005 at, as they say, the height of his powers at just 55.

I always remember him as a kind and thoughtful man with a gentle sense of humour and a palpable love of life, his family and his exceptional work/vocation/hobby.

Not only did he write most of his publications, but he delivered them himself in his little van packed with boxes of books to a host of outlets all over the county, from National Trust shops to WH Smiths branches.

He was one of a very rare and special breed of person: someone who brought delight to the hearts of strangers, both with his publications and his constant bright-eyed cheeriness. And Sally's clever design work was flawless.

Paul Theroux

In the case of my entry into the Obelisk canon: not only had I lived through many of the events, after joining the paper from the *Falmouth Packet* in 1974, but I had free rein to plunder *Advertiser* files through the auspices of its then editor George Taylor.

At the outset, I rather thoughtlessly, unfairly and uncommercially entitled my manuscript *Ugly in the Storm*. This was based on two things: the dire floods that bookended the decade and a quote from American travel writer Paul Theroux who first saw Newton Abbot from a train in 1982 on his epic coastal tour of Britain. In *The Kingdom by the Sea* he wrote: "The rain came down. We went along the north bank of the muddy Teign to Newton Abbot, which looked very ugly in the storm."

Perhaps he caught the place at the worst moment, in dreadful weather and viewed from a steamy railway carriage packed with loud-talking passengers. And the town had just been through a decade of stress, and was probably still licking its wounds: its market heart had been ripped out and re-built (not to everyone's taste) and residents were still counting the cost of a second savage flood.

Sometimes the storm of protest over some contentious local issue was as ugly as the real storm that brought inescapable unattractiveness to shops and homes.

This book is comprised of a purely arbitrary collection of events, large and small, significant and fleeting, dramatic and uncomplicated; a personal choice of what seemed interesting, important, amusing or off-beat from those ten extraordinary years. Consequently, many things are missing, some only get a passing mention whilst others engender longer passages.

The 1970s seemed to fashion much of what has become the present Newton Abbot. No doubt there are more changes to come. Will they be on the same grand scale again – and will there be more ugly storms?

Cllr Mrs Di Nicholls

Di and Bri, pictured below the historic first-floor Jacobean plasterwork ceiling of the Grade Two Old Manor House in Wolborough Street with the original title

When *Newton Abbot in the News* finally hit the book stores, my newspaper gave it a nice promotional plug and renowned local district councillor Mrs Di Nicholls posed for a snap with me signing a handful of copies she had bought for herself, family and friends.

Di featured in the book, in a photograph of the pre-Teignbridge Council steering committee of 1973 and was a fervent supporter of her electorate during her long and industrious service.

She remembered many of the incidents, including the controversial creation of a new market complex, the opening of the town bypass, the establishment of Channings Wood Prison at Denbury and – especially – the dramatic felling of the power station chimney on land across the River Lemon from Wharf Road in 1974.

Her late husband Reginald was leading driver at the power station and the Central Electricity Generating Board organised a marquee on the site to mark the demolition for CEGB chiefs, the workforce and local councillors. But when the charges were set off, the chimney did not immediately fall in the direction it was intended to go. Said Cllr Mrs Nicholls: "It wobbled. For a minute I thought it was going to topple on top of us." Fortunately it did not. But the *whump* of its collapse was so loud that it triggered a migraine and she had to go home.

Mrs Nicholls died in 2017 aged 99, just a few months short of her century and a telegram from the Queen. A staunch Labour supporter, she was known for her wry sense of humour and a relentless pursuit of truth and fairness for all. Her twenty-years-plus of civic service began in 1971 when she was elected to Newton Abbot Urban District Council. She joined the steering committee of the fledgling Teignbridge District Council in 1973 and was a member of the authority until the early nineties. She chaired its housing committee for two years and also served a term as council chairman.

She joined Newton Abbot Town Council in 1974, was its Mayor in 1985/86 and stood down in 1991. She was a familiar face in the town, always stopping to chat to pedestrians, and was also prominent as a seasonal volunteer at St Leonard's Tower on its open days; she was a Scavenger for the local Court Leet and regularly masqueraded as a French onion seller for the traditional Cheese and Onion Fayre, with a painted-on curly black moustache. She was both a governor of Bearnes Primary School and served the Feoffees of Highweek for many years.

In 2013, the same year that she joined fellow long-standing town councillor Henry Cole as an Honorary Freeman of the town, she received the British Empire Medal in the New Year's Honours List for services to the community, presented at an investiture at County Hall by the Lord Lieutenant of Devon, Eric Dancer.

Born in Torquay and a much-medalled swimmer from school age, she went to London at 18, worked in a dental practice and joined the RAF at the start of World War Two where she dealt with ammunition requisitions. Firstly billeted in Warwick, then in Okehampton, and latterly in Austria and Germany, she also wrote and presented plays for the troops, and met celebrated band leader Glenn Miller when his orchestra played at RAF Mildenhall, Suffolk, shortly before he was lost when his plane tragically disappeared over the English Channel.

She left the RAF with the rank of Corporal in 1947, began writing and performing plays with the Shiphay Amateur Dramatics group, moved to Newton Abbot with husband Reg in 1955 and joined Newton Abbot Labour Party branch. Her subsequent activities included writing letters calling for the release of Nelson Mandela and collecting food donations for British miners during their bitter strike in 1984. For her latter efforts she was presented with a miner's lamp, and on her 90th birthday she received a letter of congratulation from the then Prime Minister Gordon Brown.

Her local campaigning included securing a footbridge over the A380 to link Buckland Estate with the town centre following several pedestrian fatalities, and achieving the modernisation of council houses in Broadlands, where she later lived.

I met Di when I moved to Devon in 1975 and we retained a strong friendship over the years. Of the many anecdotes she told, this was her special favourite.

As a lifelong pedestrian and irked by the thought that many district councillors just drove around the area and had little contact with the electorate (except at election time), she once proudly and emphatically told a Teignbridge meeting that she *did* connect with ordinary people because she "walked the streets of Newton Abbot" – an unintentional *double entendre* that prompted much laughter and soon fell into district council folk lore.

The town council subsequently erected a commemorative plaque to Di in its Golden Lion Square project. It begins:

IN MEMORY OF 'DI' NICHOLLS B.E.M.
18th MAY 1918 – 30th AUGUST 2017

And it adds at its base

A TRUE LADY OF THE PEOPLE

That is what made her so special.

The Mid-Devon Advertiser

The newspaper that was to become the *Mid-Devon Advertiser* was born in Newton Abbot in 1863 – in an era of horses, carts and bicycles, and in the middle of the American Civil War.

Queen Victoria was on the throne and Lord Palmerston was Prime Minister. Albert Edward, Prince of Wales (later Edward VII) had married Princess Alexandra of Denmark (later Queen Alexandra).

The year was also notable for the opening of the first section of the London Underground, from Paddington to Farringdon Street, and the founding of the Football Association.

Amongst those destined to be famous were future British Prime Minister David Lloyd George, motor manufacturer Henry Ford and Norwegian expressionist Edvard Munch, whose painting *The Scream* reminds many of us what it feels like getting up for work in the morning.

The Newton Weekly Journal was established by printer, painter and picture-frame maker James Welford – who was proprietor, editor, reporter, compositor, reader, foreman, pressman, clerk, canvasser, stationer and bad-debt collector, with the help of just one other – in offices at 10 Queen Street, a former grocery shop.

In 1870, the short-lived Newton Abbot Newspaper Co Ltd changed the paper's name to the *East and South Devon Advertiser* and it was sold in 1876 to Daniel Vile, later to become its editor. The broadsheet then moved to premises next to the British School and changed offices yet again in 1879, to a house in Market Street.

At the time it was printed on one of the oldest presses in the west of England, an antiquated platen with a stone 'bed' worked by a weight and a lever.

In 1908, the company was sold to the Mid-Devon Newspaper Co, which would own it for the next 60 years and its title finally became the *Mid-Devon Advertiser*. A.J. Coles (Devon dialect writer Jan Stewer) was its editor from 1909-13. The Hearder family – publishers of the *Newton News and Directory* and *Hearder's Almanac* – began its connections with the business from 1920.

These ceased in 1969 when Beaverbrook Western took over the title, moving it to premises in Wharf Road. In 1976 it became part of West of England Newspapers Ltd, a subsidiary of Mirror Group Newspapers Ltd.

The masthead of the Advertiser in the 1970s. And, yes, it was 20p then…

After that it was sold to a consortium of West Country businessmen until, in 1986, it came under the Devon and Cornwall Newspapers umbrella of Tindle Newspapers Ltd.

The paper moved in 1990 to a 450-year-old Grade Two listed premises, the Old Manor House, in Wolborough Street. The medieval property – converted to accommodate newspaper offices – was built in 1534, five years before the dissolution of the monasteries.

Known then as The Great House, it was headquarters to the Abbots of Torre, who lived at Torre Abbey, Torquay, and was used mainly as a secular or civil court.

In the 19th century it housed a private school for a time and then became a residence; it was the headquarters for a car dealer, and then housed architects' offices and finally the local Royal British Legion Club before being bought in 1988 by businessman Keith Stokes-Smith, 43rd holder of the Lord of the Manorial Borough of Newton Abbot.

The Old Manor House, pictured in 1970

A facsimile of the oldest available edition of the paper, July 17, 1869, was reproduced in 1990 to celebrate the move into those premises which boasts Jacobean plasterwork, a brace of mediaeval fireplaces and a ghost (though I never knew anyone who actually saw it).

The paper's editors since Mr Coles have been Arthur Pope (to 1951), Sam Street, John Kendall, Lance Samson (1973-1993) and Tony Stevens, who retired in August 1994; Mr Stevens was succeeded by George Taylor, who was followed in an acting editorship capacity by Stephen Taylor; Ron White then became the paper's first editorial manager; he was followed by Keith Perry and Ruth Davey and the present incumbent is Nick Knight. It celebrated its 150th birthday in 2013. Previously a broadsheet publication, the paper dropped to a small tabloid size in September 1976, a dimension it retains today.

The *Advertiser* is now based in the 119-year-old former Invertère clothing premises in Courtenay Street – its public offices, news and sales on the ground floor, occupying the former YMCA charity shop premises. The renowned Invertère (Latin for "to turn about") Coat Company Limited was formed in 1904 to make innovative reversible coats.

The Queen Street offices, 1970 ; Jan Stewer (A.J. Coles); The Wharf Road building

News and advertising staff prepare for their walking entry in the 1977 town carnival. At the time the paper's suggestive tee-shirt slogan was "I GET IT EVERY FRIDAY," then its publication day. Pictured bottom right, displaying that pithy motto on her shorts, is trainee reporter Sally Russell who also capably served as Miss Teignbridge for the district council's own Teignbridge Fair in that busy Jubilee Year.

Yes, we have no tomatoes

THERE will be a slight Devonian touch to the forthcoming LP by British rock band, Yes.

The album's title will be Yes Tormato" — a name that began when the group's guitarist Steve Howe discovered Yes Tor, on Dartmoor.

LIVEN

The idyllic spot was chosen as a good location for photographs for the album's cover—but the group were later disappointed with the shots and decided to liven them up a bit by tossing tomatoes at the prints.

Naturally, the idea for the album name arose from the incident.

PRESSING

It seems odds-on that the Yes Tor pictures will indeed grace the album cover. As an Atlantic Records spokesman said: "I think they will probably have to do that to explain what the name means."

No date has been set for release of the album because of problems at a pressing plant.

About the Author

"This working journalist used to find himself in all sorts of situations, making the job (at least in my heyday) so fascinating. Sadly many regional newspaper reporters today – those still left in situ - find themselves stuck at desks, copying Twitter posts and conducting interviews via Facebook instead of venturing outside – though, thankfully, not at the *Advertiser*. In the photo above, yours truly is reporting on the just-before-deadline blaze at the Salmons Leap Restaurant just off the A38 near Buckfastleigh in August 1975.

"This was the first time I saw for myself how hard it was – even for experts – to put out a fire constantly smoldering and re-igniting under a thatched roof. It was explosive. It was also the first time I got to dictate my story on the hoof from a telephone box to meet a pressing publication deadline – after getting the low-down from the Fire Chief, that is (man in white hat). And, to make that horrible roll-neck shirt of mine even more horrible, it was orange… Also, how times change: the site is now a charging park for electric cars, alongside the new Strawberry Fields café and farm shop."

A CORNISH-BORN writer and journalist based in Devon, Brian has written extensively for newspapers in both counties, specialising in local government, face-to-face interviews and musical matters.

His varied career has included work as a school photographer in Yorkshire, several years as a local officer for the National Union of Journalists and writing private, low-key comedy shows for performance with several groups of friends.

He has provided cartoons for various publications, sung with several rock bands and was one half of an eccentric improvisational musical comedy duo with his late collaborator Pete Gretton about whom he has written a mini-biography, *Out of the Sun*, that recalls some of those unconventional artistic days.

His reporting apprenticeship at the Falmouth Packet in the early 1970s as an 'adult entrant' followed an initial six-year career as a library assistant at Falmouth Public Library and a creative stint as part of the Falmouth Packet advertising team, where he often illustrated advertisements.

Coming to Devon in 1974 he worked firstly for the weekly *Mid-Devon Advertiser* and then evening paper the *Herald Express* before returning to the *Advertiser* in 1977 and serving as its chief reporter for some twenty years from 1979 before taking early retirement.

He wrote and edited Newton Abbot's own town guide for several years and has produced a handful of books – all paperbacks and available from Amazon, as follows.

The Other Side of the Ribbon:

Real life reminiscences. A hilarious inside look at the things actually said and done in provincial newspaper news rooms. Illustrated with the author's own cartoons.

"Made me laugh out loud."
"I loved this book... howled with laughter."
"A real treat for those lucky enough to have worked on community newspapers."

Guts

A comic novel. An isolated Cornish country hotel, a dark February night, a violent winter storm, an eccentric housekeeper, nine reluctant guests and a furious company chief executive with a dead fish on his pillow. Can reporter Barry Bodkin solve the mysteries of their unexpectedly corpse-spattered weekend break?

"A rollicking read with a twist in the end that I didn't see coming! Perfect for a TV adaptation."
"An excellent read! A fascinating insight into journalistic politics and a whodunnit approach that keeps you turning the page. Highly recommended."

The Never-Ending Tales of Dara's Bar

A portmanteau novel with associated short stories. Ten story-tellers. Eleven stories. One dingy backstreet bar. A single barman. And a demoralised writer, desperate to get his creative mojo back. Can this battery of diverse adventures change his life, and how much can he reveal about his past before he can lift the pen once again?

"A real gem of a book... a wholly exceptional read... a highly individual presentation of great short stories, told in the cosy confines of a dark bar, and complete with a superb twist at the end."
"A friend gave this to me to have a read of - they added that it was very good - but that's gotta be the understatement of the year! Because this book is really a GREAT read... You gotta find out for yourself how good this book is."

Out of the Sun

An eccentric biography. The true story of Devon-based composer and psychiatric nurse Pete Gretton's life seen through the eyes of his long-time friend and collaborator. From creating original songs on any piece of equipment that might conceivably record them, to his final and more sophisticated basement studio in Devon. Packed with photographs, cartoons, song lyrics, comedy sketches, recording details, news clippings and other memorabilia.

"For anyone who knew Pete and the worlds he occupied it is a must-read… a uniquely moving and inspiring insight into what made this unsung hero tick… the kind of heartfelt tribute that could only come from a close friendship and creative partnership that spanned 40-plus years. A truly commendable tribute."

The UFO Armageddon

A small parody book. An uproarious look at UFOs, unlikely aliens and ludicrous fictional reminiscences. Illustrated with the author's cartoons it tells the story of an old, defunct flying saucer magazine allegedly created by identical twins on a work bench at the rear of their garage in the mid-1980s.

"Brilliantly funny... I find something fresh in it each time I pick it up."

When Rabbits Go Bad

A collection of comic verse, witty song lyrics and cartoons.

"A must-have collector's item. Zany creativity."

Petals

A selection of more soulful poems stretching from the 1960s to 2020.

"Words that float off the page. Enchanting, entertaining and reflective."

You can contact Brian at
ink4mation-writer@yahoo.co.uk

Want to know more about the history of Newton Abbot?
Check out the extraordinary Town and GWR museum!

Newton's Place, Wolborough Street
Newton Abbot, TQ12 1JQ
Telephone: 01626 201121
Email: museum@newtonabbot-tc.gov.uk
Further information:
https://museum-newtonabbot.org.uk/visiting/museum-access

Fully accessible
Admission Free
Opening hours: Tuesday-Friday 9.30am to 4.30pm
Saturday 9.30am to 1.30pm, Sunday and Monday Closed

Printed in Great Britain
by Amazon